A CHURCH TO COME HOME TO

A CHURCH TO COME HOME TO

by

Mary G. Durkin

and

Andrew M. Greeley

THE THOMAS MORE PRESS
Chicago, Illinois

ISBN 0-88347-141-8

TABLE OF CONTENTS

Preface, 9

PART I

PART II

I am the bread of life.
He who comes to me will never be hungry;
he who believes in me will never thirst.
But, as I have told you,
you can see me and still you do not believe.
All that the Father gives me will come to me
and whoever comes to me
I shall not turn him away;
because I have come from heaven
not to do my own will
but to do the will of the one who sent me.
Now the will of him who sent me
is that I should lose nothing
of all that he has given to me,
and that I should raise it up on the last day.
Yes, it is my Father's will
that whoever sees the Son and believes in him
shall have eternal life,
and that I shall raise him up on the last day.

(John, 35-40)

What description, then, can I find for the men
of this generation? What are they like? They
are like children shouting to one another while
they sit in the marketplace:

> "We played the pipes for you,
> and you wouldn't dance;
> We sang dirges,
> and you wouldn't cry".

For the John the Baptist comes, not eating bread,
not drinking wine, and you say, "He is possessed".
The Son of Man comes, eating and drinking, and you
say, "Look a glutton and a drunkard, a friend of
tax collectors and sinners". Yet Wisdom has been
proved right by all her children.

(Luke, 7:31-35)

PREFACE

EVERY book has its origins in the experience of the author. This study of the phenomenon of people returning to the Catholic Church is rooted in the experience both personal and professional of two authors: one a male, celibate, priest, sociologist; the other a female, wife, mother, theologian (ironically, the sociologist originally studied theology and the theologian did her undergraduate work in sociology). Though in the jargon of the sociologist we share the same "gene pool," we feel our experiences, both personal and professional, bring two different perspectives to a topic of mutual interest.

The reflections in this book use a process of pastoral theology. They are based on scholarly examinations of relevant theological and sociological material. When the sociologist uncovered the presence of a significant number of returnees to the Catholic Church, the theologian was challenged to wonder: what does our religious tradition say to their experience? We have not attempted to offer a definitive explanation of the phenomenon of the homecomer or of the possible response by the Church, but we hope to call attention to the presence of this group and to initiate a pastoral response to its presence.

Our thanks to Georgiana Duffy for her typing skills which greatly aided the task of combining the ideas of the authors.

Mary G. Durkin
Andrew M. Greeley
February 14, 1982

Part One
CHAPTER I
A Church To Come Home To

THIS is a book about people, God and the Church. It is about people given to Jesus by the Father, people Jesus does not want to lose, people Jesus wants to raise up on the last day. And this is a book about the Church, that social institution which attempts to carry on the transforming work of Jesus in every generation. It is a story of how, in this present generation, many who seek to believe in the Son are handicapped in their attempts by religious leaders who, like the men of the Lord's generation, know neither when to play the pipes or sing the dirges; and it is a story of a vision of life offered by Jesus that could enrich the lives of both the people and the Church.

Let us begin, as we must these days, with a story.

Two young assistant professors of sociology, teaching at different universities in a large city, decided to marry. Irish Catholic in background, educated in Catholic colleges, they wanted to be married in the Newman chapel at one of their universities, even though they were something less than devout, practicing Catholics. When they approached the chaplain, he demanded to know whether they were "practicing" Catholics—a question that in the strict term of canon law was none of his business. We do not know whether he asked if they were living together (which was even less his business), but he may well have, since it is a question now routinely asked by priests like him. In this particular case, we gather, the couple were not living together. The priest then informed them that since they were "fallen away" Catholics, he could not marry them unless (a) they took six instructions in the Catholic faith from him and (b) promised they would resume Sunday mass attendance immediately.

The young couple were somewhat dazed, in part because they suspected (probably correctly) that they knew more about Catholic theology than did the chaplain. They turned to a young priest at a neighboring parish who laid down no conditions, imposed no demands, asked no outrageous questions. He spent several sessions with them in informal conversation about Catholicism and helped them to prepare the liturgy for their wedding mass. So impressed were they with the sensitivity and intelligence of the young priest, that they began to go to the mass he said on Sundays to hear his sermons. An Irish Catholic like themselves (as was the Newman chaplain), the young priest gave a sermon at the wedding mass that had everyone in tears.

Needless to say, the young couple appears dutifully every Sunday morning to hear him preach and to receive Holy Communion.

There are a number of points to be noted about this story. First of all, given their backgrounds, the return of these two young people to the Church was virtually inevitable. Their decision to be married at mass, while they may at first have justified it to themselves in terms of "keeping the parents happy", was the first step in such a return.

Second, the Newman chaplain's attempt to impose harsh and extra-canonical guidelines on them was crude and unjust. Indeed, it was unjust in the strict sense of the word since canon law gave him no right to insist on the requirements he laid down.

Third, the young couple was sophisticated enough to "shop around" and search for a priest who would be less rigid in his requirements.

Fourth, the young priest was able to provide religious instruction and inspiration delicately and deftly, without having to fall back on rules, regulations and guidelines.

The story is unfortunately all too typical of a distressing phenomenon currently occuring in American Catholicism. A very large number of Catholics, particularly college educated and of Irish background, who have drifted away from the Church are now drifting back to it. The response of the organized Church is frequently authoritarian, heavy-handed and insensitive, imposing a discipline far beyond that dreamed of by even the most rigid curial canonist.

"Coming home" to the Church is a major religious and social phenomenon in American Catholic life. Perhaps as many as half the Catholic population in their early 40's have in some way or another come home to the Church. Unfortunately, the leadership of American Catholicism, including in this case even the parish clergy, are utterly unaware of the phenomenon. They are responding with the harshness of the "guidelines movement," one of the most vicious and pernicious phenomena to emerge since the last Vatican Council. It is almost as though the clergy, in substantial part responsible for having driven these Catholics away from the Church, now want to impede their return home.

A considerable amount of money and an enormous amount of energy has been poured into the subject of "evangelization" within American Catholicism in the last several years (without, be it noted, any appreciable increase in the numbers of people affiliating with the Church). In the meantime, a phenomenon far more important than the evangelizing of the unchurched (at least in terms of its numerical payoff) is the return home of those who have temporarily left. Characteristically, institutional Catholicism ignores these people or treats them like wicked little children who have to be patronized, punished and reeducated.

This book is about the Church to which the drifters come home, not about the clerical incompetents who try to prevent them from coming home. It is not designed to persuade people to come home, for the evidence suggests that those who do come home do so almost entirely of their own accord. It is rather intended to be a description of those aspects of Catholicism that attract people home—though, of course, it may appeal to those who are pondering a return.

Virtually all of the sociological assertions in Part One of this volume are based on empirical evidence collected over the last decade of studies of American Catholicism at the National Opinion Research Center (NORC). We do not intend to make this a sociological monograph. We will not disturb the reader with tables, models and quantities of statistics. The reader who is interested in documentation will find it in such volumes as *Catholic Schools in a Declining Church, Crisis of the Church, The Young Catholic Family,* the *Young Catholic Adult,* and *The Religious Imagination.*

After examining the experience of "drifting away" and "coming home" from a sociological perspective, we will then, in Part Two, try to connect the insights we discover there with our religious tradition and uncover the religious meaning from our analysis of what turns out to be an important religious experience in the lives of a sizable number of American Catholics. We will not engage in abstract theological discussion though we will seek to relate the experience of "coming home" in its various dimensions to concrete expressions of our faith found in the stories of the Scriptures, hopefully providing the basis of a vision for those who come home.

Some preliminary background information will be useful.

In the early 1960's, approximately two-thirds of

American Catholics went to church every week. By
the middle 1970's, in the wake of the encyclical letter *Humanae Vitae*, the proportion of weekly church
attenders had fallen to almost 40%. Since then,
however, attendance has increased to 52%, and
from less than 35% to more than 50% for Catholics
under 35.

The magnitude of this return has been obscured
somewhat because there have been two separate
"drift" phenomena going on since the late 1960's.
The first was the "Humanae Vitae backlash," which
hit Catholics between 25 and 40 especially hard.
Anger over the birth control encyclical was enormous, much greater than the leadership of the
Church realized or is willing to admit to itself. The
anger continues, but those who drifted away have
discovered that a majority of those who remained
affiliated with the Church are equally angry and
nonetheless feel under no constraints to cease being
active, practicing Catholics. Therefore, the
Humanae Vitae drifters are now returning in considerable numbers, accepting much of their Catholic
heritage but completely dismissing the Church's sexual ethic. *

---

*Some right-wing Catholics, most notably those associated with *The
Wanderer*, proclaimed that such "do-it-yourself Catholics" had no
right to call themselves Catholics. The fact is that, as in so many other
matters, the radical right is theologically and canonically wrong. You
cease being Catholic only when you formally renounce your

This *Humanae Vitae* drift is what social scientists would call a historic event, a one-time impact. It is not likely that the Vatican in the future, no matter how inept at decision-making, would find a way to offend, insult and hurt so many people no matter how hard it tries. Though to give Pope John Paul II proper credit, it must be said candidly that the image he has managed to create for himself as antisex and antiwomen, in the objective order, certainly looks like an attempt to drive Catholic laity away from the Church. We are well aware that what John Paul has actually said in matters of sexuality and women is very different than what is reported in the press. In later chapters we will highlight some aspects of a positive vision to be found in his statements on sexuality, work, the family and lay participation in decisions affecting their religious life. However, eventually the man must assume responsibility for his public image and the public perception of his words.

In addition to this "one-shot" drift in the Church, there has also developed a "life-cycle" drift phenomenon, in which some people in their early and middle 20's become alienated from organized religion, as they do from virtually all other organized

---

Catholicism or join another denomination. You may be a poor Catholic, a bad Catholic, a hypocritical Catholic when you reject some of the Church's teaching (although in the matter of birth control such a rejection can't apply to a teaching that has not been infallibly defined), but you are still a Catholic. The judgment about whether someone is a sinner or not is properly left to God.

social institutions. The period of "swinging singles" is not the happy, carefree, playboy/playgirl stage of life that many think. It is a lonely, isolated, uncertain time in which social institutions are viewed with suspicion. At the time of marriage a reintegration into society and its social institutions, including the Church, begins. Statistical evidence shows that a very high proportion of those who have drifted away will drift back again by their late 30's or early 40's. Indeed, Church attendance of Catholics in their early 40's is now virtually the same as that of their parents 25 years ago. (More than three-fifths of Catholics between 40 and 45 attend Church almost every week.)

This life-cycle phenomenon did not exist in the early 1960's but projections based on the present behavior of teenagers suggest that the dip in religious affiliation may be less sharp in the 1980's than it was in the 1970's and late '60's. The life-cycle drift away from the Church, especially from a large cohort of young people, tended to obscure the drift back of those who were alienated by *Humanae Vitae*. If the present trend continues, however, there should be a very substantial return to the Church—at least in raw numbers—in the next five years (always assuming that the present highly negative image of Pope John Paul II and of the Roman Curia and the American hierarchy will not interfere with the trends.)

How large will this return home be? Despite the statistics of the *Kennedy Directory*, we estimate that there are 60 million American Catholics, approx-imately one-third of whom would be concentrated in the age levels where the drift away and back is likely to occur. Probably one-quarter are affected by the phenomenon, so we are talking about some five million people. But you can depend upon it: institu-tional Catholicism in the United States is not ready for such a return, and they have so far bungled badly the possibilities inherent in it.

To conclude this analysis then, a very con-siderable number of people are "coming home" to the Church after some years of either being outside of it or on the margins of it. This "drift back" seems to be associated especially with turning points in life such as marriages, baptism, the funerals of parents, the enrollment of children in school, children's reception of the sacraments. These are milestones to which the Church already has rich liturgical responses. Unfortunately, harshness at the time of the administration of these sacraments and perfunc-tory, unimaginative, and sometimes downright ugly liturgical performance impedes the effectiveness of these responses. A hastily performed baptism, a shoddy funeral service, a dull wedding homily are in fact signs against the Holy Spirit, because they negate rich and abundant opportunities for grace.

We understand pretty well the reasons for the drift away from the Church. We will examine this in some detail in the next chapter. What we do not under-stand (although there is statistical material available to help guide us towards understanding) is why, despite all the things that are wrong with the Catholic Church, most of the drifters eventually return—some of them quite spectacularly and quite dramatically. Indeed they return in their 30's at the rate of a 2% increment per year. In subsequent chapters of this book we will examine the reasons for their return. We hope it will enlighten those who are thinking of returning and aid those ministerial personnel in the Church who care about their coming back since it will be the task of these ministers to know when to play the pipes and when to sing the dirges. Contrary to what many critics say about those who have "drifted away" it is not that these young people will not dance and will not cry; it is that they have not heard the pipes being played and the dirges being sung in such a way as to touch their own experiences.

The chapter will end as it began with a story. It is a story of a conversation between one of the authors and Father William Grogan who serves in a parish where many Catholics in their early 30's, particularly college educated Irish Catholics live. When Father Grogan was asked whether he noticed a rather dramatic return of these Catholics to Church, he replied, "Indeed yes, the Irish are falling all over themselves trying to get back into the Church. And you know the first thing they do when they come back? They complain about the changes that have occured while they were away."

"What do you tell them?" he was asked.

"I tell them," said Bill, "that it's too bad for them. They weren't here when we took the vote, so they'll have to put up with what the rest of us decided."

It's an argument the returning Irish Catholic will understand all too well.

CHAPTER II
Drifting Away

THERE are as many stories about why people leave the church and why they come back as there are individuals who have gone through this increasingly frequent process. There are some common patterns, of course, and it is about these patterns that this chapter is written. However, it is important to note at the beginning of the chapter that the patterns do not constitute "explanations" for either departure from the Church or coming home to it. Thus, there is a strong correlation between family conflict and propensity to leave the Church. But most people who grew up in families in which they have conflicts with their parents or their parents have conflicts with one another do not leave and many of those in whose families of origin we can find no traces of such behavior do leave. This chapter is written about tendencies, propensities, probabilities, and averages, and the explanations offered should not be applied to every individual case.

Nonetheless, there seems to be both an unconscious and a conscious pattern of leaving the church and a return to it. On the conscious level, there seem to be three principal reasons that people give for leaving the church, none of which, incidentally, have all that much connection with the belief in God or even in the belief in human survival after death.

The first reason that one hears is the Church's sexual teaching, especially its teaching on birth control and divorce. It often appears that it is not so much the specific stand the church takes that offends those who drift away, but rather a feeling that birth control and divorce stands represent the church's utter insensitivity to the importance of sexuality in human life, and also (especially more recently) the church's basic and fundamental opposition to the equality of women.

There is no way the church can escape the fact that most of those who have drifted away will cite the church's sexual teaching as the reason for their departure. We don't propose to suggest that the church should change its sexual teaching (though we know that remarriage after divorce was permitted in many different places in the early Middle Ages and indeed authorized by Pope Gregory in his correspondence with St. Boniface while the latter was a missionary in Germany). We also know there are other times and places—most notably 19th century France—when the church was much less vigorously insistent on its birth control teaching than it is today. However, even if one grants that there could be no doctrinal change in these areas, one still must face the fact that birth control and divorce are perceived by those who drift from the church as merely signs of the anti-sex, anti-human, anti-woman mentality which they see pervading the church. When they come back the reason is not that they think the

church has abandoned this mentality but rather that
for them the mentality has become irrelevant. *

A second reason frequently heard for drifting
away is the authoritarian style of the Church, particularly as its been experienced in the drifter's own
life; injustice, oppression, unfairness, inhumanness,
rudeness, insensitivity in Catholic schools and
parishes seem routine in the stories of the
drifters—whether those stories be personal stories or
autobiographical novels in which the authors delight
in evening the score against an oppressive church.
Unfortunately most of those stories—whether they
be in novels or simply rectory office accounts—have
the ring of truth about them. In the last days of the
counter-reformation, churches, particularly in certain
cities and certain regions of the country, were often
marked by an authoritarianism, arrogance and self-
righteousness, that would stagger the imagination. It

---

*We strongly support the traditional sexual morality for which the
teaching church stands. However, because of its failure to develop a
positive approach to sexuality and its parallel failure to provide
anything more than a "you do it because we tell you to do it" rationale
for its prohibitions, and especially because of its unwillingness to listen
to married people on the subject of the importance of sex in their marriage, the Catholic Church has absolutely no credibility as sexual
teacher today. Indeed it seems that every new pronouncement that
comes out of Rome continues to erode the small amount of credibility
the Church brings to sexual matters. Archbishop John Quinn had the
courage to say this at the synod of Bishops in Rome in 1980. His
warning fell on deaf ears.

is as though church authorities felt that they not only shared in the infallibility of the Pope but had been confirmed in grace as were the twelve apostles. In a time of heavy emphasis on the dichotomy between natural and supernatural, some church authorities felt the only access to the supernatural was through them. One of the unnoticed evil effects of this form of triumphalism was that it justified extraordinary and bizarre behavior on the part of church functionaries; they identified with the triumphant Church and felt no guilt at all running roughshod over everyone else.

Obviously such authoritariansim is currently in retreat though it still shows up often enough in the disguise of liberalism. Liberation theology can be made every bit as oppressive a teaching as devotion to the Sorrowful Mother once was, and "salvation history" can be as authoritarian as was devotion to the Miraculous Medal. So, too, guidelines for marriage can give more control over marriage than was ever intended by the most conservative Canon lawyer. Some of the authoritarian personalities in the church may have changed their tune but they still play the same instrument. Like the Grand Inquisitor they are not prepared to concede the right of people, particularly young people, to be free to make their own mistakes.

The third most frequent reason given for leaving the church is priests. There are oppressive priests, drunken priests, amorous priests, insensitive priests, cruel priests, stupid priests, nutty priests, intolerant priests, rigid priests, uncharitable priests, thoughtless priests and incompetent priests. Again most of the stories have the ring of truth about them. There seem to be no idiocies of which the clergy are incapable.

For example, on a television program the interviewer asked a priest why the church did not permit mixed marriages between Protestants and Catholics. The astonished priest responded by saying, "but of course the church permits mixed marriages. Even at the worst times of the counter-reformation Church mixed marriages were permitted."

"Oh no," said the interviewer, "it doesn't, because there is one man in our production crew who was married to a non-Catholic outside the church because the priest wouldn't let them be married in church."

Father Robert Rolle, a friend of the interviewee, was in the control room. He spun around in his chair. "Which one of you," he asked?

It was one of the sound engineers and the story was indeed exactly as the interviewer had presented it. This young man and his fiance had gone to the local parish church and the priest absolutely refused to marry them because the girl was not Catholic. There was no discussion of a dispensation or anything of the kind. The priest adamantly refused to marry them or even to talk to the young man who was not a very sophisticated Catholic; he assumed that was the reaction he would get from any priest, so he and his fiance sought out a Justice of the Peace.

Two weeks later Father Rolle presided over a validation of their marriage. He investigated their story and found it was quite literally true. The priest in question did indeed throw out of the rectory a mixed marriage couple that had the misfortune of encountering him. As far as we know he is still doing the same thing.

How many such priests there are in the American church is difficult to say. Anyone who has heard the stories of those who have drifted away, however, would be perfectly prepared to think there are many indeed, and they are doing enormous harm to the church.

However, in addition to problems with priests, authorities and sexual teaching, there is another set of more underlying dynamics at work in the drift away from the church. John Kotre, the social psychologist, in his crucially important book, *On the Border*, studied a group of young people who had sixteen years of Catholic education before going on to graduate school. Half of them were still members of the church by their own definition and the other half were not. There is little difference between the two groups' doctoral beliefs, and sexual attitudes and social orientation. But there is considerable difference in family background. Those who defined themselves as "out" of the church came from

families where there was stress and strain, either between the mother and the father or be-
tween parents and children. Those who defined
themselves as "in the church," on the other hand,
came from families where there were few such conflicts. As Kotre noted in his book, the church is a
phenomena that emits many different cues. The
cues one uses to focus are to a considerable extent a
function of the perceptive mechanism of the one doing the focusing. It is all too easy for the Church to
become your mother, and God your father, if you
take out your angers and conflicts with your parents
on God and the Church.

On a more general level one can say there also are
people who are offended by the church's teaching,
appalled by an authoritarian experience that they
have undergone, profoundly offended by the
stupidities of some of the clergy they have
encountered, and who would not dream of leaving
the church even for a single Sunday.

Somewhere in between them are those young
people who are in the college and post-college years
who drift away from the church as a kind of revolt
against family and society even if their familial relationships were relatively pleasant. As a college stu-
dent put it, "I don't go to church on Sunday now
because I don't have to. My mother and father are
not around to insist that I go. But, of course, when I
am married and have children of my own, then I will
be going to church again."

"And making them go," she was asked?

She giggled, "I hope not, but I wouldn't be surprised if I did."

From the point of view of the social science study of religion, the phenomenon of drift away from the church is not yet adequately understood. However, it does seem reasonable that in many, if not most, cases the drifters are those who have had unpleasant experiences in the church and unpleasant experiences in the family (not necessarily intensely unpleasant), and the revolt against their church and the revolt against their family tend to be linked. Or to put the matter somewhat differently, those who report that their father's and mother's approach to religion was "joyous" are most unlikely to join the ranks of the drifters.

Of course any attempt to explain "the falling away" either entirely in religious or entirely in psychological and sociological terms is bound to be inadequate. Both the personal and social experiences of the individual have to be taken into account and also the behavior and the attitudes of the church they have encountered. If one comes from a happy family and the approach to religion is joyous and one has encountered mostly good and sensitive priests, open-minded church leaders and religious functionaries who are not anti-sex or anti-human or anti-women, the chances of becoming a drifter are minimal indeed. As one's biography deviates from that ideal, however, in any one of the dimensions listed, the chances of one drifting away increases—the more intensely unpleasant are the experiences involved, the more unlikely it is that one will ever return. Some college students, who are at the fringes of their Churches and denominations, quite candidly confess that they are going through a "phase" which they know will not last. Our guess is that they will be back by their middle or late twenties, while those whose unpleasant, family or ecclesiastical experiences are more intense will begin to return in their early, middle and late thirties. However there is no empirical evidence available to confirm that hunch.

Young people also will admit that it is paradoxical they should drift from a church precisely at the time when they are agonizing over what life means. They argue that the church, insofar as they know, does not seem to be present in their lives with the kind of resources that could facilitate the solution to such questions. Ironically, the rebels of religious practice think they are revolting against parents and society even as they themselves admit the revolt is temporary. Still, they see nothing in the church of their experience which is particularly pertinent to the human problems they experience in their station in a life cycle and are not so much angry at the church, if the truth be told, as bored by it. They do not hear church authority proclaiming a vision of life that speaks to their concerns about sexuality, about marriage and the family, about work, or even, despite much talk about social justice issues, about social justice concern within the Church itself. In later chapters we will outline the basis for a Christian vision which speaks specifically to these issues as they are affecting the lives of people in their twenties, thirties and even forties.

One might add to the triad of sexuality, authority and priests, a fourth esslesiastical cause of drift—the indifference of the institutional church to young people and their problems. The church's failure to develop an adequate apostolate for teenagers and young adults in the years after the Second Vatican Council must bear some of the blame for the life cycle drift away from ecclesiastical practice that affects many young people in their early or middle twenties. Those young people who, in their past, had sufficiently pleasant religious experiences both in their family and in their parish church, are not apt to engage in a drop-out. It is perceived by many of those who do drop out in this phase of their life cycle as being a temporary departure. In addition, the church that has failed to develop any kind of meaningful ministry to young adults (who, by and large, it simply writes off) cannot escape its share of the blame for the alienation of these people. Its failure to minister to them has been more of a disaster than its failure to prepare for their return when they marry and begin to raise families.

When asked why they leave the church, drifters themselves blame the harshness and insensitivity of the church's sexual teaching, the abuse of ecclesiastical authority, the relevance of religion to their lives, harsh treatment from priests and nuns, bad sermons, religious oppression in their families (forced church attendance, for example), the oppression of women in the church, intellectual problems about the teachings, and loss of faith. (The last two, by the way, are mentioned very infrequently.)

Still, a sizable portion of these drifters will find their way back into the church despite all the things they find wrong with the Catholic Church. When and why they return, and how they are received upon their return will be examined in the following chapters.

CHAPTER III
Coming Back

DRIFTING away from the church is usually a gradual and sometimes imperceptible process. Only rarely is there a systemmatic and decisive decision. It simply happens that one day a person realizes that he or she is no longer a practicing Catholic or indeed no longer a Catholic at all. The return to the church can be equally gradual and imperceptible until suddenly one day one realizes that one is once again a Catholic and indeed very much so. As Peter H. Rossi once put it, "when I was twelve I left the church. When I was forty-five I woke up one day, looked around and found I was a Catholic again. I hadn't changed any. But without anyone telling me about it they had expanded the boundaries so far that I was inside again." The inestimable Don Pietro exaggerates, but only somewhat. Our church surely did change a lot between his twelfth and forty-fifth birthday. Also, he underwent a few changes himself.

We understand rather less about the process of return than we do about the process of departure. For some it is merely a life cycle phenomena. After a certain age, young people grow out of, transcend, or integrate or repress their conflicts with their parents and society and settle down, perhaps regretfully, to being responsible adults. Such adult responsibility involves reaffiliation with society, and reaffiliation with society normally involves becoming part of

33

some denomination. Now indeed the numbers of Americans who have no religious affiliation at all has doubled since 1960 but still represents only six percent of the population. As Will Herberg, God rest him, remarked so many years ago, "in America you have got to be *something*." By and large that "something" will at least be within your denominational tradition, so you will be, as Herberg argued so brilliantly, either a Protestant or Catholic or a Jew (within the denominations, the Episcopalians at the top of the heap and charismatic, Pentecostal and fundamentalist churches at the bottom seem to be the greatest gainers, while the mainline churches in between, especially the Methodists, are the greatest losers). For young Catholics reaffiliating with society normally means that they become Catholic again, for the other options seem even less attractive.

This reaffiliation often takes place around the time of marriage and family functions as some of the young persons decide that now they are beginning a family of their own, it is time to settle down and be serious about life and that involves having a religion again; most likely the religion in which you were raised. Indeed, the denominational reaffiliation is linked to a political affiliation. So re-integrating oneself into society for young people of Catholic background involves not only returning to the Catholic denomination but to the Democratic party. Moreover, the intensity of these two reaffiliations is also correlated—the more devout the religious behavior, the more likely one is to be a "strong" Democrat. The neighborhood wins out eventually whether one likes it or not!

This early and middle twenties life cycle, religious drift phenomenon is probably represented fairly accurately by those college students who say yes, sure they're not going to church now but when they get older, they will go back to church. For most such young people, the return is essentially a maturation phenomenon, which is not to say that the drift and the return are not important religious opportunities for the church but merely to assert that the process is relatively uncomplicated. It is part of a larger phenomenon of societal alienation and then reintegration which church leaders ought to understand and take into account in their ministry.

If marriage is the first turning point when people begin to drift back to the church, it would seem logical that the birth of children would be the second turning point. This may be the case but we have not been able to substantiate such a possibility with empirical evidence. For our respondents under thirty, there does not seem to be a correlation between return to the church and the birth of the first or a second child; for respondents over thirty, about whom we have much less information, there does not seem to be any correlation between the number of children and the return to church, at least not when age is held constant. Rather it would appear that each additional year of age increases the return to the church and that numbers of children do not seem to correlate significantly with return. It may well be, however, that the important turning point is not the birth of a child but the beginning of the child's grammar school education and the need to think seriously about providing answers to the religious questions that the child begins to ask.

Theoretically, at any rate, one might hypothesize that the next two turning points after marriage are the birth or Baptism of the child and the child's beginning grammar school education. The former, like marriage, provides a time when the church can make a direct intervention in the process of return (which it often does, it would appear, by acting unpleasantly and setting up obnoxious conditions). If the beginning of grammar school education is not necessarily a religious ritual (although it might be a quasi-religious ritual if the child is to attend a Catholic school), First Communion presumably comes shortly after the beginning of the grammar school years, and surely is another important turning point not only in the life cycle of the child but perhaps even more importantly in the life cycle of the parent. Theoretically at any rate, these might be occasions when those who have begun to drift back to the church will indeed come to the time of critical decision.

However, the empirical evidence suggests that rather more likely than a turning is simply the gradual erosion of disbelief and anger and the gradual increase of faith and the desire for religious community with each passing year of life. Here the data is at hand. We might suggest tentatively that marriage and age are the two most important phenomena leading to a drift back to the church. Marriage then ends the young adult alienations from society and age forces maturing adults to consider both the meaning of life and the implications of his/her own limitations. The church that cared about their returners—and there is no evidence whatsoever that American Catholicism gives a hoot about them—would want to study much more carefully the processes and the dynamic indications of the turning point (another name for all of which would be the "graces"). With the possibility of a Catholic's return to the faith of his or her childhood, the church that cared would wonder what moments of grace it might be missing and what opportunities for grace it might be handling badly. Concerned as it is, however, about the liberation of the Third World or new international economic order or gun control or other major issues over which it can have no control, American Catholicism is hardly likely to be even mildly inquisitive about the reasons why those who have drifted away also drift back.

If the occasion and the processes of return are unclear, the persons who influence the return are easy to determine—the spouse, the parish priest, and perhaps (at least theoretically) the child.

There is no more powerful religious influence in a

person's life than the religiousness of a person's spouse. It is very unlikely that a married person will return to the church alone. Either the couple will come back or they will not come. Moreover, both the strength of the influence and its benignity are indications of how happy and fulfilling (especially sexually fulfilling) the marriage tends to be. Fallen away Catholics who are happily married to one another are much more likely to return to church together than to return separately or not to return at all. If the church is to activate those images, those pictures, those stories, those memories of the past to attract fallen away Catholics back to the church, then it is the joint religious imagination of husband and wife which must be influenced. (As the years of marriage progress, the correlation between a husband's religious imagination and a wife's grows ever more powerful, particularly if their sexual relationship is fulfilling.) Husband and wife are the most powerful of all sacraments of grace for one another. All other influences pale in their insignificance by comparison. If the church is eager to recall those who have drifted away, then it must appeal to the marital unit, not just to one or the other spouses and it must try to facilitate the marital fulfillment and happiness of those to whom it is appealing.

We have no empirical evidence about reverse socialization—that is to say, the religious influence of children on their parents. While there is certainly a wealth of impressionistic and anecdotal information that would indicate that children can be a very powerful religious influence on their parents, it would be somewhat difficult technically (though not impossible) to measure the precise nature of this influence in empirical research. One hypothesis that ought to be tested carefully would be the assumption that a parent who was disposed to return can be easily nagged into it by vigilant and persistent children—much the way children these days nag their parents to stop smoking (another excellent example of reverse socialization).

Finally, priests have a powerful positive influence which can draw people back into the church. In our study of young adults, we discovered that those young people who describe themselves as closer to the church than they were five years ago were five times as likely as those who were still at the fringes of the church to say that they had a close personal relationship with a priest. Moreover, they were six times as likely (thirty-six percent versus six percent) to say that the sermons that they heard were excellent. For young people in their thirties, at any rate, the influence of the priest / confidant and of the priest who was an excellent preacher as a factor in leading to the return to the church is very powerful indeed. Unfortunately, young adults give priests very poor marks in both their preaching and counseling roles (the National Federation of Priests Councils—the professional association of Catholic priests—meets each year and takes global stands condemning injustices all over the world. It never, however, condemns the most ugly injustice of which priests are guilty—the injustice of not providing the laity who pay the priest's salary with the good preaching and the sympathetic listening which is their right).

All the more important, then, one must conclude, are those occasions when a person who has drifted away from the church comes in contact with a priest. Weddings, funerals, Baptisms, First Communions, Christmas, Easter, Mother's Day, and the other times of the year in which a marginal Catholic will show up in church. A priest must assume when he preaches at a wedding, funeral, Christmas, Easter or some other special event, that there will be many, many drifters in the congregation. Some of them cynical, some of them skeptical, some of them hoping and praying that the priest will show them a way back in. Anyone who has attended a Baptism or a wedding or a funeral or a Christmas or an Easter Mass will testify that many, many priests seem utterly oblivious to the opportunities in such a situation. Last Easter, for example, two Catholic colleagues told horror stories about dragging fallen away relatives to Mass on Easter Sunday. In one case the sermon was (of course) on birth control, and in the other case, the sermon was on church finances, mixed with harassment against those who only showed up for church at Easter time. You'd think we'd be happy people still cared enough to come at Easter. But no, we denounce them for being there and thus increase the probability that they won't show up at all next year at Easter.

There is a considerable wringing of hands among some of the clergy today about the declining importance of their ministry. It has been our melancholy experience that no amount of empirical evidence telling how important the role of the priest is and indeed how increasingly important it is, has any effect at all on this self pity. A very substantial number of the clergy simply do not want to hear that they are important, indeed critically important, in reclaiming the sheep that have temporarily strayed away. If you don't want to feel that your work is important, then there is nothing anybody can do to change your mind. Besides, if you are convinced that your ministry doesn't matter, then you don't have to work hard at preparing good sermons. Nonetheless, for those who have ears to hear, let them hear: the priest is tremendously important for preparing the way for those who are seeking to return to the church.

Pursuit of the "unchurched" is currently a fashionable fad in American Catholicism and "evangelization" is the watchword. One hears wild and usually undocumented statistics about how many people there are out there without any church affiliation who are hungry for religion. In fact more careful analysis of the available data shows that most of the unchurched are unchurched because they want to be unchurched and that their sexual attitudes, for example, are utterly incompatible with Catholic orthodoxy. It is a curious twist that the church is not concerned about those of its own house who have drifted away and are often trying to find a path on which they could return.

There is nothing automatic about the return of marginal Catholics. There is a powerful, statistical propensity for those who have drifted to come back. But, however powerful the propensity, each individual return is a unique experience in itself and when and whether someone returns to the household of the faith depends on highly contingent events and circumstances—the way a priest handles a marriage preparation, the sermon at the funeral of a parent, the elegance of a Baptismal ceremony, a sermon on Christmas day, a conversation on an airplane, the influence of a spouse, even the right Catholic book at the right time and place. Given the utter indifference of the church at present to those who want to return, it is astonishing that as many come back as do. Even with standard, rigid, arbitrarily hostile guidelines, if the church sets itself seriously to the task of attracting and welcoming those who have temporarily left home, the result would surely be a dramatic surge in the quantity of those who come back and also a tremendous improvement in the quality of their religious life after they come home.

People come back anyway because they want to come home. The Catholic left, concerned about the international economic order, and the Catholic right, concerned about articulating and enforcing guidelines, cannot be excused for their lack of interest in this homecoming on the grounds that they are unaware of its existence. Pastoral ministers might, quite honestly, claim they do not know how to minister to the needs of these homecomers, because they do not, for the most part, understand their needs. The task confronting the concerned pastoral minister is two-fold: (1) increase her/his understanding of the experience of those who are returning, and (2) uncover within our Catholic Christian tradition a vision that speaks to this experience.

As Mother Teresa has so often emphasized, we do the work of the Lord when we look for those within our midst who are in need of love and the offer of salvation. The homecomers will return but this return will be more of a "raising up" when pastoral ministers learn when it is appropriate to play pipes and when it is a time for dirges.

Let us now turn to a more detailed examination of five interrelated reasons why people come home to the Church.

CHAPTER IV
Heritage

IT is alleged that your man Jimmy Joyce was once asked why, if he still believed in God (which he did at least some of the time), he did not join the Church of Ireland after his apostasy from the Church of Rome. Jimmy is alleged to have responded, "Sir, I may have lost my faith; I have not lost my mind."

It was a demonstrably unecumenical statement, but then it was made in an unecumenic era. It does, however, illustrate the enormous power of the Catholic heritage even on those who have disaffiliated. *

One of the reasons for coming home to Catholicism, then, is that you have to be something, and you are certainly not likely to become a Jew, though that is, for most of those raised in Catholicism, a more appealing choice than becoming Protestant. So you return because somehow or other you are able to distinguish between that Catholic heritage and tradi-

---

*If Joyce lived today in an Irish Catholic suburban parish, he probably would have been a member, if not the president, of the parish council. When asked once, toward the end of his life, if he really was still a Catholic after all, his response was, "Ask them, don't ask me". The borders of Catholicism have been extended so much since the last Vatican Council that the Church would undoubtedly have contained him. *Finnegan's Wake*, after all, has as its underlying theme the Catholic notion, H.C.E.—"Here Comes Everyone!"

tion that you may only dimly understand and the stupidities of the Roman Curia that you have sometimes experienced in your local Church. Catholicism, you realize, has been around a long time and has done some pretty spectacular things—witness Notre Dame de Paris, *The Divine Comedy*, and the great medieval and renaissance paintings. It is a heritage of which to be proud, and it is yours. What's more, you suspect that being born a Catholic may be like being born black or a Jew or a woman: it is something that sticks with you. Furthermore, it is at least as good a religious heritage, if not better, than any of the others currently available. As Will Herberg argued, in the United States you had to be a Catholic, Protestant or Jew. The structure of our society presumes a religious affiliation. Things have not changed all that much since Herberg's time. The proportion of people who list no religious affiliation may have increased from three to four or five percent; but still, most Americans are Protestants, Catholics or Jews. If you have something, and as you become older and more integrated into society, it is reasonably clear that you have to be something, then you will likely choose your own heritage because you feel more comfortable in it, you were raised in it and because, after all, for weal or woe, it is yours. Also, despite yourself, you feel a little bit proud of it.

One of the reasons then for coming home to the Church is because it represents roots. In a society where men and women are very conscious of the importance of roots and of rediscovering their continuity with those who went before them, Catholic roots can and often do become enormously important, even though it is difficult to specify often exactly what those roots are. (All of the reasons for coming home listed in the separate chapters of this book overlap and converge. There is no particular order in our presentation of them, because no logical order presents itself. All of the reasons for coming home are part of the Catholic heritage and Catholic roots for which the homecomers are seeking.)

The search for Catholic roots is often vague, uncertain, even implicit. It goes on in the preconscious religious imagination (of which we speak more in a subsequent chapter). The art of returning to the Catholic tradition, following the Catholic heritage, exploring your Catholic roots consists essentially of being able to distinguish between those things and people in the Catholic Church you cannot stand and those other elements of Catholicism, perhaps hazy and unspecified, which you value and with which you feel at home. One of the most interesting and, in our judgment, unexpected phenomena of the last century is how many Catholics have become quite practiced at that art. They do not know quite what the Catholic heritage is, because even in education ten to twenty years ago it was not presented as well as it might have been. At the present time, with our cult of the instant moment, American Catholicism is utterly without historical awareness. No one reads Aquinas, Dante or Augustine any more, much less Hopkins, Thompson, Mauriac, Bloy, Waugh or G. K. Chesterton—at least not Catholics. Mention Henry Adams', *Mont San Michel and Chartres* to those educated in Catholic institutions and virtually all of them will look at you in bafflement. A non-Catholic may observe that it is, of course, a classic. Liberation theology, si; Henry Adams, no!

The tragedy for those who come home seeking roots is that nobody has told them how glorious and distinguished are the Catholic roots to which they are returning. American Catholicism seems to have made a pilgrimage from believing that the 13th was the greatest of centuries to thinking that there is nothing worthwhile in any of the centuries before 1950. Those who come home looking for their heritage and a tradition stumble back into a heritage that is far richer than they can imagine; but, sad to say, there is only a clergy with harsh and rigid guidelines to welcome them back, none of whom appears to appreciate or understand the richness of their tradition. (How many priests have read *Mont San Michel and Chartres* or, lacking the time, to read a book, glanced at that incredible hymn to Mary, "The Virgin and the Dynamo"?)

The Catholicism to which many are coming home is of rules and regulations, grim prohibitions and atrocious guidelines. Still they come home because they perceive that there is something more. (How they come to perceive that we shall discuss in a later chapter.) They may not even be greatly interested in adult education to enhance their understanding of heritage and tradition—especially since one cannot presently imagine more than a few adult education programs that take cognizance of, much less teach, the richness of the Catholic heritage in any detail. Yet there are ways the rich wonders of the Catholic heritage could be insinuated into their perception of the Church. One hesitates to think of the enthusiasm with which they would return to their Catholic roots if they understood fully how much those roots involve and contain.

There are two very important facts that must be kept in mind about this groping for roots which is part of coming home to the Church:

(1) The people who come home are doing so on their own terms. To put the matter bluntly, they don't give a damn about Canon Law, the Papacy, the Congregation for the Defense of the Faith, the national hierarchy or the local bishop. Having absorbed most of the stupidity and the banalities of which the institutional church is capable, these people could not care less about what the institution says and does—beyond the parish level. (They may care very much about the quality of Sunday sermons in their parishes, which in most parishes is still intolerable.) They come back to Catholicism not because of the institutional church but despite it.

They usually return with the conviction that the institutional church has absolutely nothing to say that is important for their religious or their family life. Therefore quoting papal encyclicals, hierarchical statements, episcopal letters to them only wastes time. They simply don't care about that aspect of their heritage. They want to belong to Catholicism; indeed they are determined to belong to Catholicism. They will belong on their own terms and in the way they choose, honoring the practices and the precepts they think are reasonable, acceptable and salutary. They may suffer through the foolishness of the guidelines as a necessary precondition for getting back, but that does not mean they consider the guidelines or any other rules and regulations of the institutional church to be legitimate. They are only things you have to put up with if you want to regain access to your roots.

The clergy and the right-wing laity may rant and rage about this "selective" approach to the Catholic heritage. How can you, for example, want to send your children to Catholic schools and blithely reject what the church has to say about divorce, birth control and obligations to the Third World? Maybe you can't, but people do, and they are doing it in increasing numbers. There is not a thing the authorities in the institutional church can do to change that situation, especially since they do not have either the Inquisition or the secular arm to impose their vision of Catholicism on everyone else.

One could well argue that this phenomenon of being Catholic on your own terms is new only to the United States (and perhaps to Ireland, England and Canada). Other countries such as Spain, France and Italy have known it for a long time. The special American difference, though, is that in most of the continental countries, being Catholic on your own terms means a minimum level of religious devotion and parochial involvement. In the United States, however, the "do it yourself" Catholic is very likely to be a weekly communicant and a member of the parish school board, an active, devoted and committed, though highly selective, Catholic.

(2) Once people have made the choice to come home to the church despite all its weaknesses and deficiencies, there is precious little you can do to get rid of them. They have made their decision after some considerable soul-searching and perhaps at the cost of enduring the humiliation of the guidelines. Having made the decision to return and suffering through the difficulties that are involved, they are not about to leave no matter what the provocation. The Pope may denounce them as consumerists, the Catholic right may insist that they do not belong to the church, the liturgical "purists" may bore them with dull liturgies but they have come home to their roots and they have come home to stay, and everyone from the Pope on down damn well better believe it.

We are not suggesting that those who have come

home to their roots are likely to be troublemakers. Some of them may well become involved in church organizations; the majority probably will not. They will be content, rather, with the educational and liturgical services their local parishes provide though they may shop around for the local church that seems most responsive to them. The presence of a substantial portion of these homecomers in the Sunday congregations changes the atmosphere of the institutional church and the local parish. There are a lot of folk out there on a Sunday morning who are there not because they feel they have to be there but because they want to be there. They are also there, however, on their own terms, with their own agendas, their own paradigms and their own mode of affiliation. They expect very little from the church and receive very little. This does not mean, however, that they are not grateful for understanding, sympathy, support and powerful religious motivation. As we will discuss in a later chapter, priests are one of the reasons they have come home; however, they expect little in the way of ministry from the institutional church, though they gratefully accept what little ministry they do receive. They are a challenge and an opportunity for the institutional church. Nevertheless, no matter how much the institutional church may offend, affront and short-change them, they have come home and they have come home to stay.

CHAPTER V
Values for Children

THE empirical evidence suggests that marriage and aging are the two principal correlates of coming home to the church. Marriage, particularly to another Catholic (and young people are as likely now as at any time in the past to select a born Catholic as their marriage partners; the higher rate of mixed marriages is entirely a function of lower conversion rates at the time of marriage), has a sudden and more dramatic effect on return rates.

Aging has a gradual, more long-term effect on the propensity to come home. (It should be repeated once again here that not everyone comes home, but eventually most do—for whatever encouragement that might be to parents who are troubled by the apparent apostasy of a child.) Nevertheless, many of those who do come home assert that one of their primary reasons is that they are looking for a value system that they can pass on to their children. Furthermore, those priests who are sensitive to the homecomers report that it is precisely at the time when children begin to attend grammar school that the homecomers begin to turn up on the rectory doorstep. I cannot dispute the testimony of either the homecomers or the clergy who welcome them back, but the empirical evidence does not suggest that children as such cause people to come home. More likely, the decision to come home is made at the time of marriage or with the advance of years because both of these facts involve some decision about how the children are to be raised. The fact of the decision may be revealed when the children come of school age, but the decision itself has been made to some considerable extent well before then. So children are an important part of a decision to come home, but it is a decision about passing on the values to another generation made before the actual physical presence of children.

The process seems to work something like this. Parents look around and observe that many children are raised in home environments where there are almost no explicit values and sometimes precious few implicit ones. They perceive that these children are at an enormous disadvantage as they struggle through decisions of their own maturation, looking for values and norms according to which to make decisions but finding none in their family environments. "Kids," these parents say in effect, "gotta have values. I had values when I was growing up. I may have rejected some as harsh, insensitive and irrelevant, yet growing up with them was better than growing up with no values at all. I'm not too sure what my own values are now, and I don't have a helluva lot of confidence in them, but I want to be able to pass some values on to my children. So, in the absence of anything better, I might just as well go home to the value system in which I was raised. It's changed a lot—some ways for the better and some ways not—but, as far as I can see, for all its faults, there aren't any other sets of value systems around I would prefer to pass on to my kids. Therefore, I will go home to Catholicism and try to raise them as Catholics, at least after a fashion, so they will have some of the advantages and, hopefully, less of the disadvantages that I had growing up in a Catholic environment that was drenched with Catholic values."

This ambivalence and the poignancy about the loss of the old Catholic value system is revealed in the enormous outpouring of contemporary Catholic novels. The novels rejoice that the old tyrannies are gone, that Sister Mary Holy Water, for example, no longer tells you not to wear black patent leather shoes; but they also lament that the church does not have May crownings any more.

One of the more interesting aspects of the decision to come home in order for the kids to have values is the parental assumption that the church, the parish priest and what's left of the system of Catholic schools or C.C.D.—*something or somebody* will transmit values which parents feel deficient in their abilities to transmit. In effect, parents are saying, "Look, I don't have any values any more or I'm not sure what they are. I need somebody, like the church, to come along and give my kids some values so that they have something to accept or even fight against. At least they will have a value structure to grow up with."

It is almost as though the parent is asking the

church to compensate for their own deficiencies in values.

"I'm not sure", says the parent, "exactly what Catholic values are any more. But I think it's a good thing for my kid to have some values and I don't know where else to turn for them. Of course, I may not buy the church's values for myself and I may not live according to them, but I want the church to do what it is supposed to do for my kids and teach them the values I don't think I have".

The irresponsibility in such a stand is obvious. Its futility may be somewhat less obvious. The church can at most only reinforce the values that young people acquire in their homes. It cannot compensate for parental deficiencies in values; it cannot teach how to live or why to live if children are not learning by parental rule and example, by the quality of the relationship between the two parents and by the parents' love and affection for the children. To want Catholic values for your kids when you're not willing to live by them yourself is to want the impossible. So at first blush it may seem dishonest to come home to the church in order that your children will have values that you yourself do not share.

In the real world, however, the matter is much more complicated. Oftentimes children are used as a pretext to search for values and rejuvenation that the parents also want, but they cannot or will not admit they want. Many of those who come home to the church in order that they might find values for their children also seek to rediscover values for themselves.

Moreover and more importantly, they may have many of the values they are looking for inside their personalities, their imagination, their lives. They may be far more Catholic than they realize. (Like one novelist who claims to be the worst Catholic since Ghengis Khan but whose writing is full of Catholic convictions and Catholic perspectives of which he seems to be unaware.) As we argue in a separate chapter, Catholic stories of God and stories of faith and even stories of Mary (to lift three titles from John Shea) have a way of surviving in the religious imagination and permeating the personality even when people are isolated from the church and have rejected most of their Catholic past. Values are finally pictures in the imagination that are more ultimate, more powerful and more basic than any propositional statement or ethical norm. You may repudiate the institutional church, you may reject the formal doctrinal, ethical propositions; but the pictures, stories and images remain and have an enormous impact on your life. Again, as we will note in a subsequent chapter, Catholic married people, normally without realizing what they are doing, are able to use their stories of God and stories of faith to reinforce and facilitate their marital happiness and indeed their sexual fulfillment no matter what the institutional church may say in propositional terms about sexual-marital ethics. The roots they wish to pass on to young people—that they think they no longer have—in all likelihood persist, though only dimly perceived, but nevertheless powerfully operating in the religious imagination. So, such parents expect the church to pass on values they no longer possess, but in fact, perhaps without realizing it, they expect the church to pass on values they still hold.

The process may be subtle, but it does not make it any less powerful. The parent dimly perceives, or perhaps more appropriately, vaguely imagines, a series of pictures and images which provide meaning and guidance in the art of living. The parent is not altogether sure how well he or she is doing in transmitting such values to the kids. (If the quality of intimacy between the husband and wife is good, they can almost count on it—the values are indeed being transmitted.) What the parent is really seeking—and in our judgment, legitimately seeking—is an institution which will affirm, validate and confirm the stories and pictures which by word, deed and relationship are already being transmitted in the family environment. The argument that is implicitly being followed is a legitimate probability gamble: "Maybe if I have the church telling them the same thing I'm trying to tell them, they will be more likely to listen."

It is a fair bet, because while the church often does an extremely bad conscious and explicit job in retelling its story, the stories themselves are so powerful, so attractive, so illuminating that even badly told, they have an enormous impact on the imaginative life and hence on the total life of those who hear them. If one rephrases for parents the statement that "I have come home to the church so that there will be some values to pass on to my kids," into the statement, "I have come home to the church so that the same stories I heard when I was growing up will be told to my children," then "coming home" for the sake of the kids makes a lot of sense. Parents must realize, though, that they are telling the same stories themselves.

For example, a parent in his or her early thirties, when trying to explain to a child what Christmas and Easter is all about, almost surely will tell the stories of two caves; one in which a child was born and another in which a man was reborn. Again, try as the mother (father) might, it will be very hard, if they were raised with a Catholic imagination, not to speak of the renewal of life in both caves, of birth and rebirth, of resurrection and triumph of life over death, of good over evil, love over hate, forgiveness over sin. The crucifix and the crypt, the wise men and the shepherds and Mary Magdalene coming to the tomb are stories that are hard not to tell your children at Christmas and Easter if you have been raised in the Catholic heritage. You may not be altogether sure yourself what to make of the stories, though in telling them to your children you may be astonished to discover that you still "kind of" believe.

Even though you are not quite sure how you would handle certain propositions of christology and soteriology that might be involved in those stories, nevertheless a baby was born in Bethlehem and the condition of humankind was changed; a man did die on Calvary and something wonderful did happen on Easter morning when he still lived and the change was made permanent and irrevocable. In the face of those two awesome realities, doctrinal propositions and intellectual doubt somehow seem less important. You find, as you tell these stories to your children, that while you are still not altogether sure intellectually that you believe them, in the depths of your personality and in the imagery of your preconscious, you do indeed believe that they are true in the sense that they reveal what human life means and how humans ought to live. If you tell the stories of Christmas and Easter and at least halfway believe them and halfway live their implications, then in a very fundamental, basic and pervasive sense you have transmitted the critical values to your children. You are still Catholic and they will be Catholic. It makes sense to come home to the institutional church so that the kids are raised in the presence of other people who tell and believe the same stories.

It is difficult to overestimate the importance of Christmas and Easter as value-drenched occasions. Somehow or other we have become so troubled about doctrinal propositions and citing such peripheral issues as Papal infallibility, the "real presence," or how one defines the presence of the divinity in Jesus that we miss the enormous, awesome and fundamental truths of God's love and the triumph of life over death which are contained in the Christmas and Easter stories—stories which, by the way, sufficed to hand on the Christian heritage for most of the centuries of Christian history when the formal doctrinal propositions that could pass muster at the Congregation for Defense of the Faith were literally unknown to most of those who were part of the Catholic Christian heritage.

So the search for values to transmit to one's children is an absolutely legitimate search for all parents. The mistake is not to assert that the church can transmit these values when parents no longer possess them but for parents to assume that because they are not altogether sure of how to articulate these values in propositional doctrine that they themselves have somehow or other lost them.

Oh yes, indeed, come home to Catholicism because there are the values for your children; they are ones which in their radical narrative sense you never lost yourself. They are still in your imagination and in your life, the full manger and the empty tomb.

CHAPTER VI
Aging and Death

PEOPLE grow more religious as they grow older. With a lot of qualifications, nuances and exceptions, that is a proposition of the sociology of religion about which there can be little doubt. Many sociologists write it off by saying that as people grow nearer to death the wish fulfillment says that after all there is a purpose and meaning to human life. From this arrogant perspective it is the young who see things the way they really are and the old who, because they are afraid of death, have to pretend that religion could make a contribution to human living.

An alternative perspective, which may be hard for academicians whose youth worship is stronger than that of most Americans, is that the older people get, the more experience they have, and the more they may understand what human life is all about. The research that Philip Morgan and Andrew Greeley have done indicates that older people pray more than younger people because older people are more convinced that prayer works. The usual sociological explanation for this is that older people are more likely to deceive themselves. However, as Dr. Morgan points out in his analysis of these materials, it may also be the case that older people have more opportunity to observe that in some fundamental sense prayer does work; prayer does indeed facilitate happier and healthier lives. (By the way, there is a powerful correlation between frequency of prayer and psychological well-being, as shown in our research.)

So it may not be fear, ignorance or senility that leads older people to be religious; it may just as easily be wisdom, experience and greater awareness of what life is about. The matter is certainly research-able and the presumption of the opposite explana-tion is intolerable dogmatism for a social scientist.

It is certainly true that in our research on religious practice, age is the most powerful correlate of com-ing home to the church. People who were totally alientated in their middle twenties are frequently very devout and enthusiastic participants by their early forties. Sociological scoffers are not wrong when they say that acceptance of the church is related to the increasing awareness of one's own mortality. On the contrary, as one grows older, one begins to realize that death is not just a thing that happens to some people but a thing that will happen to you, and it will happen rather sooner than you expect and rather sooner than you would like if you had a choice in the matter. One must therefore cope with the disappointments, the infirmities, the disillu-sionment, the frustrations of growing old and the implacable reality of one's death. Religion is an unquestioned aid in such coping. (Whether it is a deceptive aid or not is a matter that is utterly beyond sociological analysis, and those sociologists who imply that it is self-deception or wish fulfillment are permitting their own ideologies and their own theologies to interfere with objective analysis.)

At a certain age in life—beginning, doubtless, when one turns thirty and much more powerfully when one turns forty—one must cope intimately and profoundly with the fact that one is going to die. Indeed, research on aging done by such scholars as Liberman and Neugarten would indicate that it is during this crisis of the middle years that people attach meaning to their own deaths and then either die at once in the sense of giving up hope for the rest of their lives or continue to live in the confidence that the rest of their life is indeed vested with meaning. The struggle for meaning in the "crisis of the middle years," which herein might be defined as any time between 30 and 50, is critically important in the personal development of the human individual. In that crisis one must perforce find what one's life means, and no matter what answer one comes up with it is religious in the sense that it bestows some final, if not ultimate value, on one's existence. That most people choose an interpretation of life which says it does have meaning and purpose and fruitfulness may well be attributed to a powerful, indeed genetically programmed (*pace* Lionel Tiger) propensity. However one explains it (and an explanation by no means makes it go away), humans ordinarily respond to the harsh fact of their mortality with a mixture of fatalism and hope. Hope normally is marginally stronger than the fatalistic element.

It is as though the mixture of trials and rewards that characterizes human life is interpreted by the human organism as an indication that there are more rewards than trials finally, and that there is some purpose, apparently benign, in their lives.

Therefore, faced with the fact of their mortality, there is an inclination to become religious or to return to religion, because religion seems to offer a better explanation for what's going on in human existence than non-religion—or if not a better explanation then at least a more useful one for continuing the struggles of human life without giving up. These kinds of decisions are made not when death draws near but in the 30's and 40's, and they shape the rest of human life. But whether it be wish fulfillment or not, the inclination to become more religious in these two decades of life seems to be almost a given of the human condition. Religion helps the human personality to cope somewhat better with the facts of aging and mortality, particularly when these facts are faced clearly for the first time. It may be better, braver or tough-minded to disdain the comforts of religion and seize the ultimate end with anger or stoicism, but then again it may not.

Those who face the end with religious faith may ultimately be wiser. Empirical science cannot support either perspective. The majority of humans, however, still seem to choose the perspective of hope; and, indeed, there is no evidence to suggest they are any less likely to choose it now than any other time in human history. Hence Catholics in their 30's and 40's come home to their faith and to their church. On the whole, coming home seems to be a better way to integrate into one's personality the inevitability of death. They come home, in other words, to die, expecting to find an orientation towards death which will enable them to live the years that yet remain.

CHAPTER VII
Priests

THERE are very few Catholics either on the margins of the church or in the center, either clergy or lay, for that matter, who do not have priest horror stories to tell. Despite the enormous changes since the Second Vatican Council, the number of horror stories appears not to have declined. Incompetence, insensitivity, brutality, oppression, authoritarianism—characteristics that appear in the younger clergy as well as the older clergy, the liberal clergy and the conservative. Perhaps one should not be surprised, since the priesthood is made up of human beings; there are very likely no more unprofessional and inept priests than lawyers, doctors, dentists or psychiatrists. Unfortunately, in most other professions (and this is what makes the laity so angry) there is at least some vague correlation between performance and power and promotion. In the church that does not seem to be the case. One can be made a pastor without anyone even raising the question of whether one is capable of delivering a decent homily on Sunday.

Nevertheless, even the most rabidly anticlerical of those who have drifted to the margins of the church has a story of at least one impressive priest they have met in the course of their lives—in their parishes when they were growing up, in the high school they attended, at the Newman Club or the Catholic col-

66

lege, in the service—they have met a priest who in their minds stands for the priesthood. One of the reasons for coming home to the church is the hope of finding another such priest.

It is the supreme irony that Catholics come home to the church in substantial part because they are looking for the leadership of good priests precisely at that time when the priesthood seems paralyzed by an identity crisis in which many priests feel that, with the emergence of the deaconate and the so-called "lay ministries," the role of the priest grows ever less important in the church. This paralyzing loss of nerve in the priesthood persists despite overwhelming empirical evidence that the Sunday sermon is the most important thing the church does in the lives of its lay people. Only the spouse has greater impact on the religiousness of a Catholic adult. Priests bemoan their own declining importance and spend relatively little time preparing their Sunday sermons when in fact it is the most important thing they do—more important than it has ever been.

The desperate search of the laity for someone who can preach reasonably well often seems almost pathetic. Every time a new priest is assigned to a parish the laity collectively crosses its fingers and hopes that perhaps this will be the one who can offer, more or less regularly, a Sunday homily which provides religious illumination and renewal for their lives. Since less than one-fifth of the Catholic laity rate the quality of preaching as excellent (only one-tenth of the laity under thirty), it is evident that they are usually disappointed in their expectations. Yet they go to church and some of them come home to the church hoping against hope that they will find the priest they are looking for, the one who can comfort and challenge, reassure and motivate, disconcert and stimulate. It often seems that no matter how frustrated and discouraged the laity are in this search for priestly leadership, they continue to search—perhaps because they still have in their minds the memories of a few priests who somehow did matter in their lives.

It is difficult to sort out with the data currently available to us how important, relative to other factors, is the memory of the one or two priests who did matter and the search for another priest who might matter in a decision to come home to the church. We know that a considerable number of Catholics come home even when the local clergy make such a return difficult for them. So priests are rarely an obstacle to their return. Yet so important is the performance of parish priests in the religious identification of Catholics that the evidence forces us to conclude that the memory of the priests who did matter and the search for another priest who might matter are very important factors for many of those who come home.

On the face of it, such a conclusion might seem strange. Those who come home are probably realistic enough to know that the chances are strongly against finding a priest who might matter. They know what the odds are. Yet they continue to search for such a priest, in all likelihood because the one who did matter at some critical time in their past mattered very much indeed. He was so important, so influential, so decisive that the search for one like him, however chancey, still seems worth the effort.

What did the priest who mattered do? We have no empirical evidence to answer that question at all. Perhaps he was simply a man who could say the right thing at the right time; perhaps he himself would not remember the incident and would not comprehend how important he was in the biography of the person who remembers him as the priest who mattered. Our guess, subject to further investigation, is that he was a man who simply did his job well; that is to say, he incarnated in his personality, his words and his actions, the Catholic heritage, the Catholic perspective, the Catholic tradition, the Catholic imagination. He was, quite simply, what a priest is supposed to be: a minister of the Word and the Eucharist. He represented effectively, though however imperfectly, that which he ministered. We also suspect that the priest who mattered was most often a person of hope and encouragement, of cheerfulness and reassurance, more interested in binding up wounds than in making rules or imposing guidelines. He was a priest of whatever age who still was young and fresh in his Catholic Christian vision and communicated that vision with obvious vitality and commitment. He was a religious leader. People come home to the church hoping against hope that they will find another religious leader. For, while you can get along without them and are sometimes very happy when they go away because they can be insistent and persistent, a religious leader can be extremely important in one's life—so important that once you have fallen under the influence of religious leadership, life seemed somehow incomplete in its absence.

About ten percent of the Catholic married young adults that we have studied have what one might call a confidant relationship with a priest. Such a relationship makes little difference in terms of marital fulfillment of the couple if the confidant relationship is between the priest and the husband. But if the relationship is between the priest and the wife, this relationship enhances the sexual fulfillment of both the husband and the wife. Moreover, those people in "wife-confidant" families are more likely than others to favor the ordination of women and also more likely to want to save the continuation of compulsory celibacy—a seeming contradiction in terms, at least in terms of party-line Catholic liberalism. And it is precisely those "wife-confidant" couples in which both husband and wife report sexual fulfillment is excellent where the margin of support is for both ordained women and celibacy. It would almost seem that such couples perceive, however dimly, that it is precisely the celibacy of the priest which leads to the enhancement of their sexual relationship, and that, therefore, they have come to believe that it would be a good thing for there to be women priests so that men could also have available such cross-sexual confidants.

No claim can be made, obviously, that people come home to the church in hopes of finding a confidant who will improve the quality of their marital intimacy. We would not be surprised, however, that this factor is at work, perhaps implicitly and preconsciously, in a decision of many to come home to the church. One of the reasons that a priest once mattered is that at an earlier stage in life he may have been a trusted and, indeed, indispensible confidant. Perhaps we can find another such confidant who will help us work out the problems and difficulties that impede our marital fulfillment.

The Catholic priest is an important person in the church. He always has been and he still is, despite the resentment caused by his well-publicized resignation and despite the often self-pitying "identity crisis." There is something "mysterious" (in the good sense of the word) even "magical" (again in the good sense of the word) about priests. Priests matter. Priests matter more than anyone in the church except the spouse. Poor priestly ministry may drive people to the fringes; the ministry of a good minister makes them long to come home; and the hope that they might encounter priestly leadership with vision, taste, sensibility and courage provides powerful motivation to come home, even when one knows the odds are against finding such priestly leadership.

How many more would come home and how much deeper and richer their commitment might be once they did come home if there were more of the priestly leadership they seek? It is better not to think about questions like that too often.

CHAPTER VIII
Community

MANY Catholics drift away from the church because they find (or they found) limitations of the parish community to be intolerable. They felt it was narrow, rigid, parochial. Worse, perhaps, it was dull and middle class, parental. So they left it behind for the big world of the university or of downtown or of the swingles high rises. With the passage of time they came to yearn for something to belong to. When they drift back they hope they have come home to parishes where some of the warmth and some of the community they knew in the neighborhoods still exist.

The neighborhood parish is little regarded by Catholic intellectuals. They do not seem to realize that it is a unique phenomenon in the modern Catholic Church. It exists nowhere else in the world save in the United States and perhaps some west-of-Ireland counties. While most of us who are not intellectuals are not likely to issue calls for the abolition of the parish, we are quite unaware of its uniqueness and do not value it as one of the most effective forms of local community in the midst of urban industrial society. In the 1960's banners appeared all over convent and seminary chapels and churches exhorting us to "create community." The people who designed those banners and hung them in the sanctuaries apparently never realized that the neighborhood parish is one of the most striking manifestations of community that exists anywhere in the world—no more than those would-be members of the Catholic avant garde who celebrate the glories of the so-called "communita de basso." It would seem that if something has a foreign name and is being done anywhere else in the world but the United States it is an important ecclesiastical innovation. At a press conference during one of the synods of bishops in which a high American ecclesiastic was asked if he thought the American neighborhood parish was something like the "communita de basso," the poor man had no notion of what he was being asked.

Yet those who struggle to come home to the church, even though they have never heard of the "communita de basso" and couldn't care less about it if they had, are trying to recapture some of the neighborhood feeling of the basketball and volleyball courts, the High Club dance, the grammar school graduation—all those things that made the neighborhood parish so much a part of their lives when they were young.

Some Catholic "intellectuals" are quick to announce that the days of the neighborhood parish are over and, that with migration to the suburbs, the old neighborhood and what it stood for is finished—perhaps because they feel guilty about having deserted the old neighborhood. In fact, neighborhoods have a powerful propensity to reproduce themselves. Some of the most ardent neighborhood parishes in the history of the American Church can be found in the new suburbs. That community to which the immigrants came because there was none other available, the grandchildren of immigrants now establish by free contract. And it is for the very simple reason that, in the confused map of industrial society the neighborhood parish is a place of our own, a place where we belong and hence, most certainly, a place to come home to.

The churches in the United States have been able to maintain their claim on the loyalty of the people precisely because they remain centers for local community. The various denominations failed in Europe to bridge the gap between the agricultural and the industrial society because they were not able to transfer the community-focusing role of the rural parish into the large city. For historical reasons that are not altogether clear, this did not happen in the United States. Protestant congregations, Jewish temples and Catholic parishes managed to maintain their community center functions in the big cities and in the suburbs of the cities even better than they had in rural downstate or upstate in this country and in the peasant villages of Europe.

The local parish has been and still is a religious, social, cultural, recreational and political center. (For a more detailed analysis of the local parish and pastoral leadership in it see: *Parish, Priest and Peo-*

ple; Andrew Greeley, Mary Durkin, John Shea,
William McCready and David Tracy. Thomas More
Press, 1981.) That is the way Americans of almost
every denominational background want their local
churches to be. Indeed, the typical American cannot
imagine a local parish that doesn't play these multi-
ple roles. One of the attractions of coming home to
the church is that one will be able to come home to a
parish. In fact it is likely to be the primary attraction.
The act of rejoining the church is basically an act of
rejoining the parish—which once meant one was
given collection envelopes and now may mean that
one is given a list of guidelines.

Community is even more important to Catholics
than to Protestants. This may seem an outrageously
chauvinistic statement, but it is strongly supported by
empirical evidence. Edward Laumann, in his
research on Catholics and Protestants in both the
United States and Germany, discovered that Protestant friendship networks tend to be like the spokes of
a wheel without a rim; the networks do not close in
upon themselves in any kind of cohesive, organic
unit. But Catholic friendship networks are like the
spokes of a wheel with a rim; they are organic, structured, dense, complex, interrelated.

Catholics, moreover, are considerably less likely
to want to move from their neighborhoods or from
their cities. It has been argued that intense loyalty to
a place would be an obstacle to Catholic economic
achievement. You had to be mobile, it was said.

Like good practitioners of the Protestant ethic, you had to be willing to move, if you wanted to be successful in the American economy.

Oddly enough, the assertion seems to be true for Protestants but not for Catholics. Willingness to move does not correlate with economic achievement for Protestants, but it does correlate with economic achievement for Catholics. In other words, relative immobility is not a handicap for Catholics because there are other social mechanisms which cancel the harmful effects of geographical immobility (in all likelihood, greater ingroup loyalty).

Furthermore, as Teresa Sullivan and Joan Fee have demonstrated, young Catholic couples, during the crisis years of the first decade of marriage, are much more likely to turn to family and friends—not necessarily for explicit comfort, but at least for social support—than are their Protestant counterparts. Marital troubles, in other words, drive young Catholics to more interaction within their community networks than young non-Catholics.

These scattered research findings seem to fit together in a rather obvious pattern: Catholics are more communal, or communitarian, in their behavior patterns and more likely to set up dense, organic networks of relationships. There is considerable reason to believe that this is the Catholic interaction style, though it is less clear why that is. David Tracy has observed that in the great theological classics there is a "Catholic imagination" which is analogical and organic and a "Protestant imagination" which is dialectical. The Catholic imagination, according to Tracy, stresses ordered patterns of relationships, while the Protestant theological imagination stresses conflict, confrontation and the dissonances of human relationships. It seems reasonable to assume that the thought patterns which Tracy has discovered in theology and the interaction patterns discovered in empirical relationships have common origins in a somewhat different approach to life and to social reality between Catholics and Protestants. Be that as it may, the empirical evidence does seem to justify our saying that Catholics feel community needs somewhat more intensely than Protestants do and also seem to establish stronger community ties. Therefore, one comes home to religion, if one is Catholic (and a parallel phenomenon seems to be happening among American Protestants, though not at such a rapid rate), to reestablish the old style of human relationship one knew when one was growing up. The neighborhood parish, even the suburban neighborhood parish, apparently responds to some fairly deep-rooted needs that young Catholics acquired early in life for ordered, dense, organic human relationships.

It is also arguable that the Catholic social theory, laid down in the encyclical letter, *Quadragesimo Anno* (mostly ignored these days among Catholic activists in favor of watered-down Marxist liberation theology), is less a normative description of the way Catholics believe social reality should be organized than it is an empirical description of social reality as they have experienced it. Catholics, in other words, emphasize the importance of local community because they are more likely to have experienced it more intensely when they were growing up and more likely to need it at later periods in their lives.

So one comes home to the church seeking not only a priest who might reflect the priest who mattered from one's childhood or youth but also seeking a parish that might reflect the parish that once mattered deeply in one's life. Surely the empirical evidence is overwhelming on the importance of local parish communities in the devotional practice and church affiliation of Catholics. The better the parish—especially the parish sermon, but also a wide variety of other kinds of parish activity—the more intense will be the religious, devotional and social involvement of Catholics.

The parishes to which they come home are as uneven in their quality as are the clergy to whom they come home. Indeed, the range of parochial styles in American Catholicism is staggering, running all the way from parishes where it seems the Second Vatican Council never happened to those that are so far out one suspects they were planned by the Third or even Fourth Vatican Councils. It is certain from our research evidence that the two characteristics that Catholics most value in their parishes are activity and democracy. A parish in which nothing is happening and in which the pastor is making all the decisions is not a delight to come home to. The parish is very like the priest who staffs it in its importance to Catholics who come home. So important was parish community at one time (and since the child and the adolescent knew nothing else, they rarely realized how important it was) that the adult will come home willing to take a chance that he will find a good parish where there are good sermons, a wide variety of parish activities, sympathetic priests and democratic, open-ended parochial styles. One might call it an axiom of the coming home phenomenon that a poor preacher is better than no preacher and that a poor parish is better than no parish at all.

Just as we wonder how much easier it might be to come home and how much more fruitful the homecoming might be if the clergy were ready, receptive, even celebratory when someone came home, so we might wonder how much more joyous and fruitful the homecoming might be if the parish were structured in such a way that it would be easy, rewarding and exciting to come home to it. Obviously, the process or reintegration into the parish ought to be discreet. One could hardly list in the Sunday Bulletin all those who came home last month. The wise clergy and the wise laity should realize, however, that people are coming home, particularly in those parishes where there are many married people between 30 and 45, and that the sacramental interludes—Baptism, First Communion, Confirmation, marriages, funerals—are especially appropriate times to facilitate and celebrate homecoming. One might also add to that list the quasisacramental time of grade school graduation.

A wise clergy and a wise laity should be aware of the fact that in many, many parishes there are considerable numbers of people who are looking for a good excuse to come home. The assumption of this book is that eventually they will come home anyway, but the sooner they get there, the better. However gracious and graceful is the homecoming, the richer their religious life is likely to be and the greater also their contribution to the church. Homecoming is a special grace moment in the life cycle of someone who has drifted away, a moment for which any decently functioning parish ought to be prepared.

As far as we know, there are no parishes yet that have reputations for being good places to come home to. But it would be easy for clergy and laity to develop such reputations for their parishes, a lot easier, a lot less expensive and a lot less trouble than that caused by the pseudo-evangelism campaigns that have afflicted American Catholicism in recent years.

In some parishes, it seems to us, where the demographic situations are most appropriate, arranging homecoming experiences that are fruitful and gracious must necessarily be high on the agendas of the most important activities of the parishes. One need not engage in any theology of cheap grace to suggest that a parish which develops skills in welcoming back the homecomers will be richly rewarded. In those who are graceful, grace will be given.

Any attempts by individual ministers or by parish communities to develop welcoming back skills must be rooted in both the experience of those coming home and in the Catholic Christian tradition to which they are returning. In the remaining chapters of this book we will consider six inter-related areas of concern in the lives of homecomers and the way in which a Catholic vision of life might respond to these concerns.

Part II

CHAPTER IX
A Vision To Come Home To

IN religious language we would say that homecomers are looking for salvation, though the individuals themselves might not use such language. The movement towards reintegration into society, a link with one's roots, values for one's children, an understanding of the meaning of death and a religious leader and community to assist in the search are experiences which indicate that people are looking for "something more" than they have been able to find in the ordinary realm of their secular existence. The stories of the two caves, the cave at Bethlehem and the cave in the Garden on Easter morn, are stories about extraordinary events which hold promise that the ordinary events of our lives have meaning and purpose. The images called to mind by the Christmas Story tell us of the love of a man and a woman and their joy over the birth of a child, about the surprise of poor, lowly shepherds disturbed from their nightly slumber, about the fear of a ruler confronted with the wondrous possibility of a small baby, about the determination of Wise Men who see their research through to completion and about the worries a mother and a father experience when confronted with the threat to the well-being of their small child. Love, joy, surprise, bureaucratic fear, wisdom and parental worry are transformed in the Christmas Story into occasions in which God enters into the experience of humankind with the promise of salvation.

So, too, the events of Holy Week that lead up to the discovery of the empty cave on Easter morn remind us that, in spite of the frailties of human nature and the inevitable experience of death, there is a hope. Here, again, God is present in the common experience of death with the promise of the grace of redemption.

And it is because the Catholic Christian tradition, despite its historical shortcomings, continues to proclaim a message of hope that we have the experience of homecoming. The priest who preaches a message of hope, the religious community that is different because its members are hopeful, the religious education system which supports parents as they struggle to pass this hopefulness on to their children—all attract those whose roots are in the Catholic Christian tradition but, for one reason or another, have drifted away.

An important component of the Christian message which is especially attractive to home-comers is the promise of forgiveness. As people settle down in life and reintegrate into society, they become painfully aware of their past failures. As one woman in her mid 30's, a product of the 60's, remarked commenting on something she had done some five years before, observed, "I'd like to say that I did it with the best of intentions, but lately I've become skeptical about many of the things I did in the past." The homecomers, like many of those who never drifted away, find the guilt accompanying the recognition of our own wrong-doing debilitating and welcome the image of a God who forgives. They can even begin to forgive themselves when they hear how willing God has always been to forgive humankind for its shortcomings. The relationship of Yahweh to Israel, the Prodigal Son story and Jesus' continual forgiveness of his disciples for their foolishness and their denial of him appeal to anyone who is able to acknowledge his/her own sinfulness.

Salvation, hope, the grace of redemption, sin, forgiveness of sin, all components of the Christian belief system, when experienced not as abstract parts of a theological system but as images and stories of a warm, passionate, forgiving God hold tremendous appeal for many who have drifted away and are at a point in life where they are experiencing a need for "something more." Indeed, the sociological evidence would seem to indicate that these concepts rather than moral pronouncements and discussions over theological detail are what bring most people back.

Our analysis of the reasons for coming home reveals a fact which undoubtedly applies equally to most of those who have never drifted away (save for the small minority who are personally involved in the function of the official Church or in the study of theology). The Catholic Christian faith exercises its greatest appeal when it offers a vision of life, when it inspires people to hope that with God's help they might transform their experiences and their world, when it uses the images and stories of its rich tradition to encourage people to the extraordinary behavior called for by Jesus in the Sermon on the Mount, and when it offers the hope of God's "enspiriting" us so we will be enabled individually and as a community to continue the transformative work of Jesus, that is, continue to offer his message of hope to others.

The pages of the Old and New Testament abound with stories of people searching for salvation and of God's presence in the midst of their joys and their sorrows, their good times and their bad times. The lives of ordinary people become extraordinary through the presence of God. The problems and possibilities present in experiences of marriage and family life, human sexuality, work and commitment to religious community are part of the life of the Biblical people as much as they are part of our experience today. God's presence in the Biblical stories, challenging people to live a life according to the Divine plan and not simply according to the way of the world, is a presence which the Church needs to offer to people at all times.

Indeed, the Church is the social institution entrusted with the task of carrying on the transformative mission of Jesus, that is, to present a vision that will inspire people to live lives according to the Divine plan. We are not simply to follow rules, regulations and guidelines because they are required for membership in a social institution, but we are to commit ourself to developing an appreciation of how in our own life best to live according to the Divine plan.

Old Testament prophets proclaimed vision to people who had lost sight of God's original plan and were seeking salvation in earthly power. Jesus condemned this desire for earthly power as well as the hope that adherance to rules alone, to the Law, would assure salvation. His vision called people beyond an understanding of life rooted only in the things of this world and an understanding of religion rooted only in the Law. He continually urged his followers and all who listened to him to understand God's plan and live their life according to this.

Thus it would seem that the Church's primary concern should be with keeping the vision of Jesus alive in the lives of individuals and communities. (This does not negate the importance of creeds, doctrines, theologies and morality but maintains that objectifying abstractions seldom appeal to the experience of people's lives.)

Drifters, as we have indicated previously, will come home in large numbers no matter what the official Church does. It is quite possible, however, that many who have drifted away could be enticed

to come home more readily if the vision of life proclaimed in the Bible is articulated in such a way that it
speaks to the critical experiences of their lives.
Individual pastoral ministers, local Church communities, Bishops' national conferences, synods,
councils and even a Pope who eagerly seek the
return of those who have drifted away will attempt to
proclaim this vision. Homecomers who sense there
is "something more" in their religious tradition than
they find in their secular experience might want to
examine the stories of God, of faith and of Mary (as
we noted earlier found so eloquently presented in
the work of John Shea) and discover in them a
vision of life which speaks to their adult experiences
in a way comparable to how the stories of the two
caves impressed them as children and lured them
back to the Church of their youth.

In the following chapters we will touch on certain
critical areas in the lives of homecomers and attempt
to discern how the Catholic Christian tradition, its
images and stories, provides a vision which might
assist people as they try to deal with these situations,
as they try to come to the Son so that he might raise
them up on the last day. The vision we develop out
of the foundations of our Catholic Christian belief
system seeks to capture the creative imagination so
the drifters and homecomers will hear pipes played
for them, so they will be able to dance; and when
they need to cry, they will have a religious community
that appreciates the meaning of a dirge.

CHAPTER X
A Vision of Sexuality

IT is difficult to think of an experience of greater importance in the lives of the drifters and homecomers than the experience of human sexuality, of the possibilities and problems they encounter in the fact that human beings come in male and female varieties.* Sexuality, which is more than sex, affects every aspect of our life but is particularly obvious in certain areas of behavior: how we give and receive affection, our bodily self-images, our understanding of male/female roles, our expectations for family life styles and roles, the ways in which we are able to educate our children in sexuality, our erotic behavior, and the reproduction of the human race. Indeed, sexuality is so all pervasive that Pope John Paul II in his weekly audience addresses on a theology of sexuality and the body maintains that "it is a basic fact of human existence that at every time and every place God created man male and female." And it is our responsibility to discern and judge, again at every time and every place, who

---

*There is an overlap between the various areas of human experience included in our discussion of a Vision to Come Home To. This will be especially evident as we see how the experience of human sexuality and our understanding of its significance in the Divine plan affects the other components of the vision we will consider.

"he" is for "her" and who "she" is for "him".**

As we noted in the previous section of the book, many who drifted away because of what they perceived to be an insensitivity on the part of the Church on almost all aspects of human sexuality, and those who are returning have, for the most part, given up any hope of expecting a positive perspective on the use of their human sexuality from Church authorities. This results in a dichotomy between the official Church and many of its members, a dichotomy which often robs the Church membership of its chance to understand the Divine plan for human sexuality. Homecomers aware of the stories of the two caves often, on their own, are able dimly to perceive a vision of sexuality connected with these stories. But most of them seldom, if ever, will encounter a religious leader who will assist in the process of uncovering the Divine plan in human sexuality in the basic beliefs of the Catholic Christian system, especially as they are found in the images and stories of the Bible.

It is almost as if the homecomers, who want to come home to the Father through the Son, are never able to hear of the Son and learn of the

---

**For a more detailed analysis of these Papal audience addresses to which we will refer throughout this discussion of a Vision to Come Home to, see Mary G. Durkin, *Reflections on Intimacy and Sexuality: Biblical and Spiritual Insights Based on John Paul II's Weekly Audiences* (Alba House Cassettes, 1981), and *The Sexual Feast: John Paul II on Human Intimacy.*

Father's plan because of obstacles set up by the church whose responsibility it is to continue the mission of Jesus. Our age is not unlike that of the followers of Jesus. Religious authorities caught up in rules encouraged people to ask Jesus specific questions about moral behavior. For example, "Is it unlawful for a man to divorce his wife?" (Matthew 19, 3ff). The Lord's response to these particular questions, just as his response would be to our questions today, while not ignoring the validity of the law against divorce, directed his listeners to consider God's plan as found in the beginning stories of scripture.

Homecomers are at a particular stage in their life cycle development where they are very much like the followers of Jesus. Confused over issues of sexual identity and human intimacy, people in their late twenties, thirties and early forties are particularly aware of the problems and possibilities of the various dimensions of sexuality. And the vision of human sexuality offered by the secular society is, for the most part, a flattened-out vision which attempts to render sexuality into an ordinary, scientifically studied phenomena with no ultimate implications. Yet the lived experience of human existence as male or female often confronts people in this life-cycle stage with the issue of ultimacy. Integrating all of the dimensions of human sexuality into one's personality so as to be able to grow in one's own sexual identity and eventually share that identity with another in a relationship of intimacy, including sexual intimacy, is no easy task. Few people are able to exercise consistent control over their behavior in each of the areas of human sexuality and integrate this behavior into a satisfying, whole sexual identity. The person who never falls back on sexual stereotypes, is at complete ease with his ber bodily image, easily accepts changing husband/wife relationship patterns, has no hang-ups on giving and receiving affection, would receive an "A" as a sex educator for her/his child, is always in complete control of his/her erotic behavior and is absolutely certain about the correct decision on reproduction simply does not exist. Inconsistencies abound when we reflect on our own behavior and on the behavior of those around us.

Such inconsistencies are not at all difficult to understand when we consider the history of our sexuality. For most of human history, the primary emphasis on male/female behavior and on the relationship between the sexes has been focused on the need for reproduction of the species, a need which required that erotic behavior, that is, the strong sexual attraction, be subordinated to the species and societal need for survival. So, rules and regulations, societal and religious, dictated correct male/female roles and the female/male relationship. In a modern technological society, where there no longer is this need to encourage reproduction, societal control of erotic behavior no longer has reproductive ability as its motiviating force. When people are confronted with the question, "why male and female," they might easily say that in the past there were male and female to assure the continuation of the species, but now it would seem that the emphasis could be placed much more heavily on the bonding aspects of the relationship. But there are those in our society who would offer another vision, that is, one which would also eliminate the importance of the bonding aspect of human sexuality. This vision emphasizes solely the pleasure of the moment, thereby ignoring the importance the bonding aspect has played in the development of the species, an importance physical and cultural anthropologists and others tell us that was essential to the survival of *Homo Sapiens.*

Certainly the power of the sexual attraction has not been ignored by our secular society. The "sex sells" approach of advertising gives ample proof that even though Church authorities tend to overlook the importance of sexuality as an extraordinary experience in people's lives, the media recognizes the powerful hold sex and sexuality has for the population. David Tracy, the theologian, has said that sexuality appears to be the last great outpost of the extraordinary in our lives. And though it would seem that much of the media portrayal of sexuality tends to render it ordinary, in fact those responsible for making decisions on the use of sexuality as an attraction recognize, at least at some level, the extraordinary power of human sexuality.

Homecomers, then, are faced with many questions about sexual identity and about human intimacy. Depending on their age and family situation they are making decisions related to their sexuality with little help from their religious authorities other than guidelines and rules which continue to focus primarily on reproduction control and erotic behavior subjected to some imagined ideal of reproduction and family size. The other areas of our lives affected by our sexuality are seldom considered as a concern in Church pronouncements on sexuality.

So, the homecomers, like most other Catholics, no longer look to Church authority for help in the process of forming a mature sexual identity and entering into relationships of sexual intimacy. The influence of a secular society on this area of their life combined with the insensitivity of most Church pronouncements regarding their experiences of sexuality has tended to rob this experience of its extraordinary possibilities, that is, to deprive it of its possibility as an experience of grace, an experience of the Divine presence in their lives and in the world.

There is, however, for those whose creative imaginations have been touched by the story of the two caves, the possibility of discovering a link between the two caves and the story of creation in the Garden; this link offers a way of discovering a religious answer to the question of "why male and female," which goes far beyond a need for reproduction; which, in fact, emphasizes the importance of the bonding aspect for a real understanding of the significance and meaning of human sexuality.

A brief summary of the Pope's developing theology of the body and sexuality points the way towards a vision of human sexuality which illuminates the experience so it becomes difficult ever again to consider it simply ordinary.

Briefly, we can summarize the Pope's analysis of the story of creation found in the first and second book of Genesis: God created us male and female so we might learn to be lovers as God is a Lover and thus bring holiness into the world through our bodies. We were made in the image and likeness of God, male and female. An image reflects the model that it mirrors and so in an ideal female / male relationship we would uncover hints about the God who created us, about the Divine plan for human existence. In the "ideal" situation of the story of Genesis I and II, positive possibilities of sexual pluralism are revealed and affirmed. Alone in the Garden neither the male or the female could fully reflect God. By joining two different ways of being human into a unity of two in one flesh, the man and the woman were able to celebrate the first feast of humanity as is shown when Adam proclaims, "This is bone of my bones and flesh of my flesh" (Genesis 2:23). The first man and woman discover each other's uniqueness as a person and are able to share their personhood with each other as unselfish gift, unashamed of their nakedness, because they recognize in their interior beings, in their "hearts", the unity planned by God. They are able to exist this way in the Genesis story because they fully participate in the plan of God. They are graced and they are cooperating with God's gift of love. So it is that with the help of the Lord they are able to cooperate in the reproduction of the image of God in the procreation of new human beings. The Genesis writers, particularly the Yahwist writer of the second book of Genesis, use the analogy of what they saw as the possibility of a male/female relationship to reveal something about God and about God's plan for human sexuality.

The writer also realized that in the real experience of those who listened to the story, just as in our experience, no male/female relationship reaches this ideal. The Yahwist writer explains this fall from the ideal as a result of our free choice to eat of the fruit of the tree of the knowledge of good and evil with the end result that we live no longer within the things of the Father but we lust instead after the things of the world (I John), the world of the tree of the knowledge of good and evil. And in this world the male/female relationship, which ideally is a relationship of mutual gift, is turned into a relationship of appropriation where, in the course of human history, the male tended to lord it over his wife and she experienced desire for her husband (Genesis 3:16). A relationship of two persons is changed into a relationship of subject and object and the man and the woman are no longer able to participate in the gift of love experienced in the Garden. The shame which we experience over misuse of our human sexuality, however, is a reminder, according to the Papal analysis, of the fact that there is a plan of God which we should emulate.

Since we can no longer participate in God's original plan, are we subjected to constant experiences of shame with no hope for salvation in this basic aspect of our human experience? Here is where the stories of the caves give a resounding, "no"! They offer us the hope that the grace of redemption is in fact the same as the grace of creation and offer us a possibility of working toward fulfilling the Divine plan. To illustrate this hope, the Pope concentrates on the Sermon on the Mount, specifically Matthew 5:27-28, "You have heard it said that you should not commit adultery. But I say to you any man who looks at a woman lustfully has already committed adultery with her in his heart." Once again Jesus maintains that strict adherance to the law against adultery is not enough to transform human experience. We must go beyond the rule mentality and seek to use our sexuality as a way of affirming the personhood of the other rather than a way of simply satisfying our own bodily sexual needs. We are, the Pope emphasizes, to discern and judge "in our hearts" what is appropriate behavior to achieve this goal. We are to work in conjunction with moralists to arrive at better understanding of how it is possible for men and women to gain control over their sexual drive so it might serve its original purpose of bringing holiness into the world.

Christ promises us "the redemption of the body"; St. Paul, in his various discussions of the things of the flesh, the things of the world and our bodies as temples of the Holy Spirit, explains how it is possible for us to practice "purity of heart" (Matthew 5:8) as opposed to "adultery in the heart" (Matthew 5:28) and control "our bodies in holiness and honor" (I Thess. 4:3-5). When we allow the Holy Spirit to bring the grace of redemption to our spirit, then we are able to live a life that reflects the fruit of the spirit including joy, peace, patience, kindness, goodness, faithfulness, gentleness and self-control as opposed to a life that leads to the works of the flesh including fornication, impurity, licentiousness, idolatry, sorcery, enmity, strife, jealousy, anger, selfishness, dissension, party spirit, envy, drunkenness, carousing and the like (Gal. 5:19-23).

The God we find in the story of the two caves is also present in the story of the Garden and in the story of our own "hearts." Homecomers need to hear these stories told with the same attractiveness the story of the two caves held for them in their youth.

In developing a vision of human sexuality we have elaborated on the basic components of our creed: God the creator, Jesus the Incarnate God and

Redeemer and the Holy Spirit. The doctrines of grace, sin and forgiveness have also been fleshed out by reference to the stories of our faith found in the Scriptures. There is a positive vision of human sexuality found in our religious tradition, rooted in the stories of our faith and an essential part of the doctrines of our creed. Drifters and homecomers will hear these stories when there is a concerted effort on the part of pastoral ministers and religious communities to use these stories to help uncover the extraordinary dimension of human sexuality. There are grace-filled possibilities in masculinity and femininity. There is the possibility of the revelation of God in an experience of our human sexuality.

Unfortunately the negative image of human sexuality so long emphasized by the Church makes the proclamation of a positive vision a difficult task. In addition, human sexuality is one area of our experience that is extremely difficult to handle in an emotion-free atmosphere (not that it should be entirely emotion-free if we hope to speak to the imagination of those who will hear the stories). Many pastoral ministers are so uncertain about their own sexual identity that they are afraid to address the issue with the people they serve, or they transfer their own sexual hang-ups onto the people in the community and maintain that they could never address the topic of sexuality in a religious situation. One member of a pastoral staff rejected the possibility of using sexuality as one of the themes for Holy

Week (we die to our abuse of our sexuality in order to rise again on Easter Sunday with a transformed sexual identity) by maintaining that we would insult the people in the parish if we mentioned sexuality during Holy Week. Other pastoral ministers dealing with poor and other oppressed groups in society will claim that there are more important issues to address before dealing with what the Pope himself maintains is "the basic fact of human existence."

The strong reluctance on the part of many pastoral ministers to deal with issues of sexuality is linked to a certain degree with the fact that, for most people, sexuality equals sex and we don't talk about sex. But, for others, the all encompassing aspects of sexuality present a threat because they challenge the Church's traditional treatment of women and of marital roles as well as the pastoral minister's own bodily self-image and ability to give and receive affection.

The Catholic Christian tradition offers a positive view of human sexuality which could help people transform their own personal experience of sexuality and perhaps contribute to a societal re-evaluation of its image of sexuality. The recognition on the part of many of the homecomers of the pervasive aspects of their sexuality offers the Church leaders at all levels an opportunity to consider this positive vision. For the present time, at least as far as most of the homecomers and many of those who never drifted away are concerned, the Catholic Christian religious leadership offers no help in dealing with the complex problems and possibilities of their masculinity and femininity. It is difficult to imagine how this impasse can be overcome. Perhaps if the homecomers become more vocal about their search some pastoral ministers will respond. We hesitate to hold our breath, but we hope in the promise of the Father.

CHAPTER XI
A Vision of Marriage

THE occasion of a wedding, as we noted in the opening story of this book, often is the time when the Church has the opportunity to respond to the young adult's new-found need to be integrated into society and to have religion as an aid in this reintegration process. Unfortunately many of these young people are rebuffed by pastoral leaders, both lay and clergy, who, concerned over the rising divorce rate, have pushed for the enactment of "guidelines for marriage" in many dioceses. (For a critique of this guideline approach see Mary G. Durkin, "And They Become One Flesh", in *Tomorrow's Church: What's Ahead for American Catholics,* ed. Edward C. Herr, Thomas More Press.)

This insensitivity to the grace of the moment seems to pervade the official Church response to the experience of marriage in the contemporary world. Moral pronouncements are handed down from on high with little if any consideration of the actual experience of married life. Attempts are being made to offer support to separated and divorced Catholics, a group largely ignored in the past, but there is little effort given over to the development and articulation of a positive vision of marital intimacy which will speak both to those who are embarking on a marital journey and to those who are encountering obstacles as they attempt to live out their marital commitment. Though many married homecomers might be seeking to come to the Father through Jesus, they do not hear the message of Jesus telling them of God's presence in their daily experiences of marital intimacy.

Marriage in a modern technological society where couples can increasingly expect their marriages to last fifty or more years is an entirely new phenomenon in the history of humankind. Though married couples in previous eras of human history undoubtedly achieved marital intimacy, the span of life in which they were able to share their identities with each other in these relationships of intimacy was very short. Even intolerable relationships could be maintained for the short period of many marriages in the past. So, too, economic necessity and the care of children often demanded an unbreakable marital bond (though in many instances this did not always mean marital faithfulness). Today many women are able to survive economically on their own and raise children without the "protection" offered by the male in past eras. Also, until two hundred years ago, out of seven live births a mother and father might expect two teen-age children, whereas today in our technological society, seven live births will most often result in seven adult children. Rules and regulations about moral behavior relevant to marriage have developed out of a mentality that ignores the difference in the experience of marriage today and the experience of marriage through most of human history.

Now, more than ever, the demands placed on a married couple seeking to grow in a relationship of intimacy, call for a religious understanding of marriage. There is a need for a consideration of marriage within the broader vision of the meaning of life uncovered in a religious tradition. The popular press, which continually offers advice on how to improve a marital relationship, also encourages the individuals within a marital relationship to develop their potential, thus causing what seems to be an insurmountable tension in the ongoing journey of marital intimacy. Faithfulness and life-long commitment seem impossible dreams to many in this stage of the life cycle. (For a more detailed analysis of the journey of marital intimacy and the Catholic Christian response to this, see Joan M. Anzia and Mary G. Durkin, *Marital Intimacy: A Catholic Perspective;* Andrews and McMeel.)

Yet our Catholic Christian tradition in its images and stories is filled with material that contributes to a vision which would speak to the tensions inevitably encountered in a search for marital intimacy. These tensions, when acknowledged, can, in fact, be the impetus for a new spurt of growth in a marital relationship. But few Catholics hear this marvelous vision calling them to join their search for intimacy with the search for God to which they have been called by Jesus. Guidelines are substituted for vision, most often by people who have no appreciation for the visionary aspects of their religious heritage or little understanding of the day-to-day experiences of marital life.

The Bible is filled with stories of God the Creator, Jesus the Redeemer and the Holy Spirit joining with the human spirit so the fruits of the Divine Spirit will continually be present in the world. Many of these Bibical stories emphasize the relationship of intimacy between God and humankind and offer a model for human behavior in relationships of intimacy. When married couples are encouraged to consider the story of their marriage and live that story within the larger story of God and humankind, they can begin to appreciate how Jesus makes use of their relationship of intimacy in marriage as a way of raising them up to the Father.

The great love affair between Adam and Eve and Yahweh-God was severly tested when Adam and Eve chose to eat of the fruit of the tree of the knowledge of good and evil. They had come to take Yahweh-God for granted and wanted something more; they wanted to be God. This something more led them to the point where they almost cut God out of their hearts and hid from Yahweh-God in shame. Their rejection of God, though it damaged the God/human relationship, did not completely destroy it because Yahweh-God still loved them and wanted their love in return. So the Divine promise was made to work with Adam and Eve in rebuilding the God/human relationship. They were still to continue the Divine plan for the world and human existence, though under less idyllic conditions. Adam and Eve were able to begin anew in a relationship with Yahweh-God despite the devastation they had wrought by their earlier rejection, because Yahweh-God was a loving, passionate, forgiving God.

The numerous stories of Yahweh's relationship with Israel, beginning almost at the beginning when Moses descends from Mount Sinai and finds the Israelites worshipping the golden calf, also tell of the problems of intimacies. Yahweh-God loved Israel, as the Prophets said, with the faithfulness of a spouse. Israel, though initially responding positively to Yahweh's various offers of love, eventually became bored or wanted earthly power or things other than those Yahweh offered. At these times the Prophets describe Israel as the woman who has rejected her faithful lover or even as a whore. Yet, the lover/God continually pursued the beloved, Israel (Hosea, Ezekiel).

Married couples in their late twenties, thirties and early forties attest to the fact that their relationships have periods of ups and downs, times when one or the other is sorely tempted to walk out, to ignore the promise and commitment of faithfulness. The understanding of intimacy found in the Bibical stories offers an ideal toward which a couple might be encouraged to strive, an ideal in which the hurt and rejected partner (and in most marital quarrels both partners are hurt and rejected) is willing to take the first step towards reconciliation.

The relationships of intimacy between Jesus and his disciples and between St. Paul and the converts of his various churches also offer examples of how the ups and downs of an intimacy relationship are often opportunities for marital partners to grow in their love for each other rather than indications that the marriage is falling apart. At times, all that seems to keep a marital relationship together is the knowledge that we are bound by the command to love our spouse as ourself. This command often can help partners (at least those who are capable of entering into intimacy relationships) over the inevitable rough spots of their journey of marital intimacy.

The image of two in one flesh and of a man and woman cleaving to each other as the way in which God intended that holiness should enter the world reminds us that the Yahwist author of the Genesis story undoubtedly was familiar with a marital relationship which at some time or the other caused him to realize that a perfect relationship between a man and a woman would reflect God. For, as the later Genesis I author puts it more theologically, "two in one flesh" allowed Adam and Eve to be "in the image of God." If marital partners can be encouraged to appreciate that the way in which they live out their relationship of marital intimacy brings God into their world and reflects Divinity to those they encounter, they will have a challenge that will encourage them to work through the various social, psychological and sexual obstacles to their quest for marital intimacy.

This quest for marital intimacy in the modern world is, in the final analysis, a religious quest. It is a quest for God and a quest which needs God's continual presence if it is to be successful. Guidelines and moral regulations which fail to take into account the experience of marital intimacy as it is being lived in a particular society will result in a breakdown of communication between those who wish to enforce the guidelines and rules and those who are looking for a religious vision to guide them in their search for marital intimacy. Few, if any, homecomers hear their pastoral leaders proclaiming a positive vision of the religio-psycho-socio-sexual experience of marital intimacy. Here, too, some might on their own find the story of the two caves, a story of birth and rebirth, of death and resurrection, an inspiration for their married life. Their homecoming can be even more rewarding if, upon their return, they are offered a vision of how God is revealed continually in their journey of marital intimacy.

CHAPTER XII
A Vision of Family

THE opening scene in the movie, *I Never Sang for My Father*, showing a picture of a father and son from a family album along with a commentator's words, "Death ends a life but a relationship lives on," sets the stage for a story that captures the influence of family on all of us. For weal or woe, we all have some link, however tenuous, with our families, even when we are physically and / or psychologically distanced from other family members, even separated by death.

Richard Leakey, the archeologist, in his analysis of the remains of some of our hominid ancestors, maintains that very early on in human history a male and female who had entered into "an economic contract in which the product was children" (the male makes a commitment to care for the female whose well-being is necessary for the survival of their joint offspring), formed some sort of an emotional bond. Indeed, primatologists and physical and cultural anthropologists tell us that this love relationship which developed between the male and the female was necessary in order to insure the survival of the species, *homo sapiens*. The man and the woman became bonded to each other and, in turn, they bound their offspring to them. The offspring, needing the parents for survival, became emotionally dependent on them. And once we humans

109

became emotionally involved, we began to experience family relationships as possibilities for great joy and for great sorrow.

Those Catholics who have drifted away from the Church and those who are coming home, like all other humans, experience many situations within their family relationships which lead them to ponder "what's it all about?" They have left mother and father, perhaps to cleave to a wife or husband or maybe simply to establish their own independence. Some of them, in turn, have become the mother and father who, in the not too far distant future, will be left by their offspring. But, as the movie, "I Never Sang for My Father" so poignantly reminds us, the "leaving" does not end the relationship. Who our father and mother are and what their marital relationship was strongly influences our own identity as a woman or a man, our expectation of how a man or woman should act and our anticipation of how marital partners relate to each other. So, even though we may never consciously acknowledge this, the family of our birth plays a crucial role in our adult life. Sometimes when this role is destructive of our ability to enter into relationships with others it is imperative that we bring to our consciousness how the familial influences have affected us.

Many homecomers who are reintegrating into society, often at the time of marriage, also are confronted with the need to establish adult relationships with their parents, a situation that is often not easy for either the homecomer or the parent. While the younger person is, in fact, accepting many of the parent's values, the interpretation of what is appropriate behavior based on these values often is different for the younger person than it was for the parent. Also, the younger person's attitude toward the parents during the period of separation from society and the Church often has caused bad feelings on both parts. And, like the young person we referred to earlier, the homecomer might feel skepticism about her / his behavior and possibly even guilt over heartaches suffered by the parents. In many families the decision of the young adult to reintegrate into society is a time to begin the process of healing wounds.

Certainly there seems no better Scriptural story than that of the Prodigal Son to help in this healing process. So often the young person finds it difficult to believe that a parent will ever forgive them for their past transgressions. They do not believe that the parent could have continued to love them thoughout their rebellious period. Perhaps, if they begin to believe that they are truly loved by God and forgiven by Divine Love just as the Prodigal Son was forgiven, they will be encouraged to initiate the process of developing an adult relationship with their parents.

We indicated in our analysis of why people come home that one very important reason people return to the faith of their youth is the desire to pass values on to their children. As John Shea has said: "Passing on religion is the way we love the next generation." It seems to be part of the experience of parents as they watch their children grow that their children need values. This experience perhaps is not unlike that which led the Yahwist author to describe the generation of the first human being in Genesis 4:1-2 where we read that Adam knew Eve and she gave birth to a son proclaiming, "I have gotten a man with the help of the Lord." In Pope John II's analysis of this particular selection from the Yahwist writing he observes that in the act of procreation we cooperate (with the help of the Lord) with God in the creation of a new human being made "in the image of God." Giving values to our children, loving the next generation, getting a man with the help of the Lord, procreating a new "image of God" are all ways of capturing the experience of many homecomers who find parenthood or the prospect of parenthood confronting them with the realization that there is "something more" to life than they are able to find in their secular experience.

Research evidence shows that young people who perceive their parents as having a loving relationship are more apt to be religious than those who don't. The parents' ability to grow in intimacy is a crucial factor in their ability to give values to their children. Working toward developing a "two in one flesh" relationship in which parents are striving to be lovers as God is Lover seems to be imperative for parents who want to give values to their children.

Theresa Sullivan's analysis of the study of young adult Catholics indicates that they do not have a so-called "contraceptive mentality." They like children and have positive feelings towards having children. Their decisions to regulate births are made out of a concern for the next generation; Church rules forbiding any artificial means of birth regulation and arguments in favor of natural family planning as a way of developing self control, seem foreign to their experience of marriage and family life. Undoubtedly there are some who make decisions on family size based on selfish reasons. But those who are coming home to the Church are looking for a vision of parenthood that will help them love the next generation. If young couples can be encouraged to view the procreative task as that of working "with the help of the Lord" to continue to bring holiness into the world through the child who is in the image of God, they will be aided in the task of parenting those children.

A portion of those who are coming home to the Church—those in their late thirties and early forties—often refer to themselves as the "caught in the middle" generation. Family life, for them, seems to be one series of crises after another; crises with teenage children and crises with aging parents coupled with inevitable low points in their own marital relationships. The teenager seeking independence still is sufficiently self-centered to be unable to realize the demands aging grandparents make on their children. At the same time, aging parents fail to consider the demands children are making on their parents' time. Gatherings of people in this age bracket often turn into sharings of our tales of woe. The bumper sticker "Get Even, Live Long Enough to be a Burden to Your Children" sums up the frustration these people are experiencing. Their parents' aging is a vivid reminder of their own mortality and their child's search for independence is a challenge to their need to be generative individuals. Caught in this bind many homecomers need the assurance that fallibility in their dealings with both their parents and their children is understandable.

All of us are guilty, from time to time, of breaking the first commandment and the "strange God" that we would put before our God is ourselves. We expect that we can solve all the crises of human existence, but in order to do this, unlike Yahweh, we are tempted to do away with the freedom of the other individual, especially in dealing with our teenagers and college age children. Any vision of parenthood and "letting go" can find support in the Yahwist story of Adam and Eve and Yahweh-God in the Garden where the humans were given the choice of whether to accept what Yahweh-God (the father-mother) knew was best for them or to choose the fruit of the forbidden tree. This story coupled with the many Scriptural stories on the forgiving nature of our God and finally with the central theme of our religious tradition, that of death and resurrection, gives parents the hope that even though their children make mistakes during their teen years, there is always God's promise of forgiveness and the hope of rebirth and resurrection.

As we noted earlier, many homecomers have returned to the Church in order to deal with the question of death and then get on with the business of living. The prospect of death that becomes more vivid as they deal with changes in their parents' behavior is an important religious question in the lives of homecomers in this age bracket. There is some fear that a parent will die before the son or daughter has made peace with the parent. In other instances people find it extremely difficult to observe deterioration in the parent who has been one's role model; "if it can happen to him, then it can happen to me." The Catholic Christian tradition with its belief that if we die with Christ we will rise with him to everlasting life, the story of Holy Week and Easter Sunday, the story of Peter asking, "Lord, to whom shall we go," the story of the birds of the air and the lilies of the field, all reaffirm God's support of the human propensity to hope. The emotional burden of caring for an aging parent can be lightened when we have come to grips with our own inevitable death. Though the demands of the aging parent may continue, their threat to our existence is not a barrier to our ability to respond in a reasonable way.

Family bonds, as we have seen, bring with them questions of meaning. There are important questions in the family bonds of the homecomers, questions which probably have influenced their decision to come home. Our religious tradition with its sacramental emphasis on Baptism, Marriage, Sacrament of the Sick and the Liturgy for Death and Burial recognizes the importance of family and familial bonds. The task for the people of Christ who want to welcome those who are coming back into the community is to link the vision that grows out of this sacramental understanding of family life to the everyday occurances within a family. It is these ordinary experiences that often lead one or all the members of a family to ask the question of ultimacy, a question which looks for a religious answer.

Again, the homecomers will come home no matter what. Their lives and the lives of the entire religious community could be enriched if those issues of family life which set them wondering about the "meaning of life" are addressed on a more regular basis by pastoral ministers at every level of Church. Pronouncements, programs and proclamations about moral behavior without a vision of family life as the place where a man and a woman "with the help of the Lord" help a new "image of God" bring holiness into the world will have little effect on the future of the family or the Church.

A story of men in a parish engaged in a "renewal" program illustrates how religious leaders often miss the point on family life issues. An evening of commitment, a Pentecost, was to follow the mens' renewal weekends. The pastor had to call about half of the men who had been on the weekends but had failed to sign up for the Pentecost service (most said their wives had threatened them with divorce if they signed up for another activity outside of the home). At the service, man after man making the commitment pledge, promised to "make more time to be with my family" or "to be a better husband and father." The pastor, short on ministerial staff, had hoped that many of the men would pledge service to the parish. He was disappointed in the small number who responded to what he saw as an important need in the parish. In the process he missed the loud and clear message the men were giving him: when they reflected on their relationship with God on the retreat weekend, they recognized the need to improve their family relationships. They were asking their pastoral leader to help them in this area of their lives.

When family members are aware that God is waiting to be discovered in their relationships with each other, they will be encouraged to work at improving these relationships. The God they discover there will not be content to remain within the confines of the family but will push the family boundaries to include others who need the revelation of God's presence in the world.

CHAPTER XIII
A Vision of Work

MANY of the homecomers who were part of the rebellion of the late sixties and the early seventies find that the process of reintegration into society also leads to a degree of involvement in the world of work which they would have thoroughly rejected during their period of rebellion. Indeed, many of those who "dropped out" of society came from upper middle-class families where they felt their parents', especially their father's, commitment to work robbed the family of many opportunities for enjoyment of life. They vowed that they would never be caught up in the work syndrome; there was more to life than work and they intended to escape the tyranny of work and enjoy life to its fullest. Yet many who "dropped out" and are now reintegrating into society have discovered that work is an essential component of this reintegration. They still might not want their work commitment to be so overpowering that it robs them of participation in family life, but they are faced with the dilemma of how to put work in its proper perspective.

This need to develop a proper perspective on work is essential for all those who are in a stage of their life cycle where they are coming home to their religious roots. What is the meaning of work in the life of a human being? What is the value of the particular work that I do—for me, for my family and for my society? How do I make a commitment to work that will not interfere with my commitment to my family? Is financial reward sufficient satisfaction for the work that I do or do I need to experience personal satisfaction as well? In a modern technological society is there any value or need for individual creative endeavors? Is the work of the unpaid mother in the home of comparable value to the paid labor of her husband and other women in the marketplace? These and numerous other questions plague everyone in our society and are of particular significance in the lives of those who have drifted away and are now coming home to the Church.

The family lives of those who are coming home are being strongly affected by the influx of women into the work place. Some of the younger women are torn between the desire to gain credentials and establish themselves in careers and the desire to marry and have children. They are beginning to realize that all of their adult life will not be involved in child rearing activities. They will need some expertise for the time when they will return to the work place after their children are independent, but they are confronted with the problem of a society that does not allow people easily to move back and forth between the market place and the home. Other women feel the pressure for two incomes to maintain a standard of living (and not always the high standard of living portrayed in many articles about successful two-career couples). These women find themselves forced to return to work much sooner after the birth of a child than they would want to if it weren't for economic necessity. How are they to develop a proper perspective on the role of work?

Perhaps, not surprisingly, a technological society which provides its members with increasing opportunities for leisure time also is plagued with questions about the role of work in the lives of the people in the society. Political and economic debates about problems of unemployment, guaranteed minimum wage, wage and price control, social security benefits for homemakers, etc. are indications of the variety of visions about the place of work in human society. Few, if any, of the solutions proposed by various debaters fully answer the question of why humans work. Certainly individuals who are struggling to develop a proper perspective for their own lives on the issue of work eventually need to face the question of the basic relationship between work and human existence. They also need to deal with the fact that individual human experiences of work often fall short of what they would consider an ideal. In other words, the human situation of work is another indication of the need for redemption. We need to transform the inadequacies of our work experience and develop a response to it that will allow us to find God's presence in the midst of our work. We need to allow Jesus to use our work experience as a way of raising us up to the Father. We need a vision of work, growing out of our religious tradition, and its images and stories, that will challenge us in our own experiences and uncover the God waiting to be revealed in those experiences.

Pope John Paul II in his encyclical, *Laborem Exercems (On Human Work)* celebrating the ninetieth anniversary of Leo the XIII's *Rerum Novarum*, offers some insights that help us uncover a vision of work in our religious tradition, a vision that might need to be translated before it can address specific questions raised by individual problems of work. Still it is a vision that points to the plan of the Father, especially as this plan is revealed anew in the stories of the Old and New Testament.

Some criticism has been leveled against this encyclical because of its supposed emphasis on women remaining in the home, its failure to use non-sexist language, and the fact that, in many instances, the Church itself fails to assure the rights of its own workers consistent with the principles set forth in the encyclical. For these reasons many pastoral workers, without even reading the encyclical, are rejecting it as a viable document. Part of the argument on justice for Church workers certainly is valid at all levels of the organizational Church. It is also true that no effort seems to have been made to deal with the question of language. As the opening words of the encyclical indicate, "Through work *man* must earn *his* daily bread and contribute to the continual advance of science and technology and, above all, to elevating unceasingly the cultural and moral level of the society in which *he* lives in community with those who belong to the same family (italics for emphasis)." Seldom does a "she" or "her" appear in the entire encyclical.

The encyclical's observations on woman's role however is in the context of a call for a *family wage* and does not maintain that woman *must* remain in the home. The popular media's interpretation of these words as anti-woman, calls for a consideration of the exact words of these two paragraphs:

> Experience confirms that there must be a *social reevaluation of the mother's role*, of the toil connected with it, and of the need the children have for care, love and affection in order that they may develop into responsible, morally and religiously mature and psychologically stable persons. It will redound to the credit of society to make it possible for a mother—without inhibiting her freedom, without psychological or practical discrimination, and without penalizing her as compared with other women—to devote herself to taking care of her children and educating them in accordance with their needs, which vary with age. Having to abandon these tasks in order to take up paid work outside the home is wrong from the point of view of the good of society and of the family when it contradicts or hinders these primary goals of the mission of a mother.

In this context it should be emphasized that, on a more general level, the whole labor process must be organized and adapted in such a way as to respect the requirement of the person and his or her forms of life, above all life in the home, taking into account the individual's age and sex. It is a fact in many societies women work in nearly *every* sector of life. But it is fitting that they should be able to fulfill their tasks *in accordance with their own nature*, without being discriminated against and without being excluded from jobs for which they are capable, but also not without lack of respect for their family aspirations and for their specific role in contributing, together with men, to the good of society. The *true advancement of women* requires that labor should be structured in such a way that women do not have to pay for their advancement by abandoning what is specific to them and at the expense of the family, in which women as mothers have an irreplaceable role.

(Pope John Paul II, *Laborem Excerems* SEC IV:19. Italics in original document.)

This understanding of the need to reorder the labor process to accomodate the true advancement of women is rooted in the understanding of work the Pope finds in his analysis of the original Divine plan for human existence applied to the situation of many women in the modern world. Such an analysis does not deserve the accusation that it is anti-woman. Despite the shortcomings of the male-oriented language and of the institutional Church in its treatment of its own workers, the vision outlined by the Pope offers those who find their roots in the Catholic heritage a vision of work which might help them gain a personal perspective on the role of work in their own lives and in their society.

A brief summary of the vision of work outlined in the Papal encyclical would run something like this: from the very beginning humans are called to work since, as the Genesis story tells us, we are made in the image and likeness of God and placed in the visible universe in order to subdue the earth; work is one of the characteristics that distinguishes man from the rest of creation; when Adam and Eve are told to be fruitful and multiply and fill the earth and subdue it, we find that humans are in the image of God partly through the mandate received from the Creator to subdue and dominate the earth; when we carry out this mandate, we reflect the very action of the Creator of the universe; each and every person at every period of human history takes part in the process whereby humans "subdue the earth" through their work, giving work an objective sense.

However, the primary basis for the value of work is the human being who is the subject of the work since, as the image of God, the person has a tendency to self-realization. Work is a good thing for humans, a good thing for our humanity, because, through work, we not only transform nature for our own needs but also achieve fulfillment as a human being becoming, in a sense, more of a human being through our work. We are cooperating with the original Divine plan that we should subdue the earth and have dominion over it.

Specifically, in part five of the encyclical, the Pope outlines the elements for a spirituality of work since he believes it is the Church's duty to form such a spirituality. This he hopes will help all people find God through work by participation in God's specific plan for humans and for the world. The main points the Pope considers in his elements for a spirituality of work flow from an interpretation of the stories of Scripture concerning creation, the Old and New Testament traditions, the Incarnation and the teachings of Christ, the Cross and Resurrection and the development of the Kingdom of God through the power of the Holy Spirit.

Briefly elaborated, these elements evolve into a spirtuality that finds the "first Gospel of Work" in the stories of the first chapters of Genesis where God worked for six days and rested on the seventh showing us that the dignity of work consists in imitating God the creator in working because we alone have the unique characteristic of likeness to God. We should imitate God both in working and in resting since God performed creative activity both while working and resting. And Christ reminds us that the Creator is still working by sustaining the world in its existence and through the salvific power working in the hearts of all humans. Our work cannot consist in mere exercise in external action but must leave room for us eventually to participate in the "rest" that the Lord has reserved for his servants and friends. We are not deterred by the Christian message from building up the world but are called upon to be concerned for the welfare of our fellow human beings and to contribute to developing the world in which we live (*Gaudium et Spes*).

The Gospel of Work was continued by Jesus who was himself a man of work. His teachings continued the fundamental truth about work which had been expressed in the tradition of the Old Testament—in which we find many references to human work, to individual professions exercised by men and to the work of women. In the Parables of the Kingdom Jesus constantly refers to human work. He also compares the apostolate to the manual work of harvesters or fishermen and includes references to various forms of women's work and to the work of scholars.

So too, the teachings of St. Paul are in compliment to the Gospel of Work we find in the life and parables of Jesus. Paul boasts of his working ability and the fact that, even while an Apostle, he was able to earn his own bread. He exhorts and commands his converts to work and encourages them to work heartily "as serving the Lord and not men knowing that from the Lord you will receive your inheritance as your reward" (Col. 3:23-24).

In the Christian vision of life we find a Gospel of Work which emphasizes that the value of human work is not primarily the kind of work being done but the fact that the one who is doing it is a person, and that, although humans are destined for work, work is "for the human" and not "the human for work." Answers to many of the ethical questions we confront in decisions about work, for the Christian, include a consideration of how—in our work—we best fulfill this Gospel of Work.

However, we all know that our work falls short of the goal of complete cooperation with God in continuing the Divine plan. The original blessing of work found in the mystery of creation, when we were in the image of God, has become, in our own experience, overshadowed by the curse of toil which sin brought into our lives (Genesis 3:17). We toil until our death. Here, again, we can turn to the story of the cave on Easter Sunday and to the story of the cross on which Christ was elevated and died in order that he might return to his disciples in the resurrection with the power of the Holy Spirit. If we can unite the toil of our work with Christ crucified for us, we are cooperating with him in the redemption of humanity. In our work we find a small part of the cross of Christ, but in it we can also find a glimmer of rebirth of the "new heaven and new earth" in which we can participate through the toil that goes with work. Though earthly progress is not the same as the growth of Christ's kingdom, the fruit of human work contributes to the growth of a new human family which is some kind of a foreshadowing of a new age (*Gaudium et Spes*).

The Pope concludes the encyclical with these words: "Let the Christian who listens to the word of the living God, uniting work with prayer, know the place that his work has not only in *earthly progress* but also in *the development* of the kingdom of God, to which we are all called through the power of the Holy Spirit and through the Word of the Gospel." This vision of work does not give specific answers to the questions raised in the work experience of the homecomer but it does invite the homecomer and those who are preaching the Good News to the homecomer to develop answers to the questions in light of a consideration of work as a participation in the Divine Plan and a means of building the earth and developing the Kingdom of God. Though the homecomer individually could find it difficult to apply this vision to a specific work situation, it might be possible for those who have similar questions to evaluate their situation in light of this understanding of the meaning of work.

We are made in the image of God. The fact that we are able to work means we are capable, through our work, of reflecting God, the God we discover in the toil of our work and in the hope that our work contributes to the human dominion over the earth originally planned by Yahweh. Homecomers who are concerned about questions of work might, by vocalizing their concerns, increase the Church's understanding of how specific work situations help humans discover God's presence and reveal God to those around them.

CHAPTER XIV
Women Revealing God

ONE aspect of the institutional Church that the homecomer will find virtually unchanged is that of the influence of women in key areas of decision making processes. Although some women have moved beyond the "woman's work" of the altar society and sacristy care roles of the past, women have not come "a long way" in the Church in the modern world. Indeed, as the numbers of religious women decrease, some could argue that woman's influence in the organizational Church has also decreased. Many religious women, in the past, were highly influential in the development of the religious life of the members of the parishes, hospitals and social service agencies where they served.

Other social institutions are caught up in the dilemma of how to integrate women into key roles. Many of the homecomers have felt the tension of the societal change brought about by woman's ability to participate in the world of work and marry and raise a family. Some women might justifiably feel that the progress of women in their particular area of interest has not been as rapid as they would want it to be. However, the homecomer will soon realize that the institutional Church is caught in a bind on the question of the ordination of women. (Is it a theologically or culturally based tradition?) Other social institutions might not yet even have women in key roles, but they are able at least to maintain the illusion of openness to women with the theoretical claim that when a qualified woman seeks the role she will be considered for the position. The Church, by maintaining that women are not qualified for the priesthood—thus also disqualifying them for the position of Bishop, Cardinal and even Pope—finds it increasingly difficult to convince its younger members that it recognizes the importance of woman's contribution to the human enterprise except in family related matters.

The barring of women from key decision making positions within the hierarchial Church, which *de facto* results from their exclusion from ordination, has a trickle-down effect for all other areas of Church life. Although women today are active as lectors, commentators, extraordinary ministers of communion, religious education coordinators, sometimes even as pastoral associates, in most instances both the clergy and the laity consider them less informed and less important—thus also less influential—when it comes to decisions about matters of religion. For those for whom sexual stereotyping has become a way of avoiding the need to relate to people as individual persons, the non-ordination of women reinforces this use of a barrier to intimacy. Both men and women who are frightened by the changes in society and family life brought about by women's liberation from a life-long bond to only her own home find little challenge to their fear from the practices of the organized Church.

A particularly unfortunate side effect of the institutional Church's attitudes on women during much of its past history has been the loss of an appreciation of the womanly side of God. Though the Yahwist religious tradition in both its Jewish roots and its Christian expansion has been largely a patriarchal religion viewing God as a male father, there are instances in both the Old and New Testament and in the history of Catholic Christianity where the understanding of God, as reflected in those that he created in his image male *and* female, has been recaptured. The Wisdom that has been "proved right by all *her* children" has been seen as revealing of God. But for the most part the feminine experience has not been considered a source of Divine revelation.

At the present time there does not seem to be much hope for an imminent change in the official Church position on ordination. Still, we should not allow the successes or failures of the campaign for the ordination of women to interfere with the crucial need to understand the experience of women if we are to know more fully the God who made us in the Divine image female *and* male. Certainly the authors of the first and second chapter of the Book of Genesis recognize the importance of sexual pluralism and the experience of sexuality for the discovery and revelation of God. Pope John Paul II in his audience talks, at least, acknowledges that one human alone could not adequately reflect Divinity; it was only with the discovery of another person as "bone of my bones and flesh of my flesh" that the first humans, man and woman, could mirror God in whose image they were created. Sexual pluralism is a continual reminder of the pluralism of Divinity: the unity of "two in one flesh" is a reminder of the need to understand the experience of each individual within that unity as well as what is necessary for them to succeed in unity, if we are to appreciate the wonder of our God.

The sociological analysis referred to in the opening chapter of this book offers some beginning insights into the relationship between our images of God as mother and our religious behavior. Though the percentage of young American Catholics who say they are extremely likely to imagine God as a "mother" is low (10%), men who had a womanly image of God were seen to be more likely than men who did not have that image to imagine God as a Lover, to pray often, to offer prayers of gratitude, to consider a life of social concern and involvement to be important, to say that their sexual fulfillment in marriage is excellent, and to be in marriges in which both husband and wife report that sexual fulfillment is excellent. So, the empirical evidence supports a need to emphasize the womanly dimensions of God, at least from the perspective of young adult Catholic males.

Viewing God as mother is also an important influence on the religious lives of young women; but not as significant as it is for men. Still, we can at least hypothesize that a woman's self-image and ability to use her creative talents in a constructive way would improve if she were to begin to recognize that her experiences as a woman contribute to a deeper understanding of the God whom she images.

The difficulties in a theoretical discussion of the womanly side of God is evident whenever someone in a small or large gathering refers to God as "she." The laughter in response to such a reference reflects the newness of the idea as well as the confusion we all have with the fact that humans come in a male and female variety. A female image of God shatters some of our deepest stereotypes.

The argument here is based on the Genesis story of humans created "in the image of God male *and* female" and the need to understand the female experience to more fully appreciate Divinity. This call for an understanding of woman's experience is, at the same time, linked with the need for better understanding of the male's experience. False images of God that have developed out of over emphasis on a "macho" interpretation of the male experience need to be recognized, and their influence in the creation of a male-only hierarchical structure must be evaluated.

One obstacle we encounter when we attempt to expand our vision of God to include womanly dimensions is the argument over how much of woman's experience is based on nature and how much is based on culture. We are not advocating a complete dichotomy between the male and female experience. We see the words, "bone of my bones and flesh of my flesh" as an indication that there is homogeneity in the male and the female experience of humanity. However, as we consider human history, we know that the experience of woman in that history, and in the evolutionary beginnings of the species, has been strongly influenced by her childbearing ability. Her experience of what it means to be a human being has been different than the male experience. Now, in an advanced technological society, there are more opportunities for men and women to have similar experiences not related to the physical survival needs of the culture. But the genetic make-up of these men and women in the evolutionary beginning of the species has influenced how each has in some way differently experienced what it means to be a human person. Men and women today are strongly influenced by the history of masculinity and femininity as well as by the bodily heritage which in the past so strongly conditioned how they experienced the meaning of human existence.

Emphasizing the need to understand the female experience in order to develop a better appreciation of the womanly side of God does not mean that the difference between men and women makes one or the other inferior. As the Pope indicates in his analysis of the third chapter of Genesis, Adam and Eve's choice "for the things of the world" changed their relationship from one of mutual gift to one of appropriation where Adam, the husband, lorded it over his wife, and Eve, the woman, desired her husband (Genesis 3:16). The realities of the patriarchal society in which the Yahwist author was situated obviously influenced some of the negative interpretations of woman that followed on the story of the fall. But still, it appears the Yahwist author recognizes that this type of relationship of appropriation was contrary to the relationship of gift planned by God and described in Genesis 2:18-25. Both the man and the woman suffer in a relationship of appropriation.

Societal and religious traditions, when they encourage the continuation of relationships of appropriation, fail to appreciate the original Divine plan for man and woman where, through the unity of their differences, they reflect the God in whose image they are made. Unfortunately, in the development of cultures in which the males' ability to "lord it over" the female became more powerfully entrenched, woman's experience came to be considered inferior, an inapporpriate source of imagery about God.

Though there are certain positive references to women in the Old Testament, the culture of the periods in which these books were written considered women inferior. The stories of Jesus' relationship and treatment of women point toward his wish to include the role of woman among those

aspects of human society which would be transformed by the grace of redemption. Still, the view
of woman presented in both the Old and the New
Testament is an interpretation of her experience
through the eyes of the male author (though one
Biblical scholar maintains that the Song of Songs
might easily have been written by a woman). Thus it
is not always easy for women who encounter
Mystery in their experiences of life readily to connect
this with the stories of their religious tradition.

Julian of Norwich is an example of a mystic who
experienced God directly as "our mother": "As truly
as God is our Father, so truly is God our mother."
She also referred to Jesus as mother since she felt
Jesus represented the womanly characteristics of
God. Some observers of the devotion to the Blessed
Mother believe that this devotion grew in its intensity
as a way of expressing the feminine dimension of
God. (For more detailed discussion of this see
Andrew M. Greeley, *The Mary Myth*, Seabury.)
While this might be true at a popular level, some
women commentators believe that the Fathers of the
Church set Mary apart from other females and
honored her as one who did not share the corrup-
tion of womankind. Still, stories of Mary are being
re-thought as a way to encourage women to
recognize the revelation power of their experiences.

Even in the time of the "world of the knowledge of
good and of evil" women's experiences, as well as
men's, offer us a possibility for interaction with

Divinity. As the Biblical scholar, Roland Murphy, observes in his analysis of the wisdom literature of the Old Testament, this literature provides a Biblical model for understanding Divine revelation through a dialogue with Divintiy "which takes place essentially via human experience and creation . . . (where) the Israelite encountered in the Lord a vital faith relationship which is as valuable as the liturgical experience in the Temple, or the exodus event itself." Though Jesus Christ is central in the redemptive plan of God, Divine presence and revelation are diffused in the world. Reflection on experiences of women could lead to a deeper appreciation of the God who we believe has revealed more of Divinity in the mystery of Christ, but who established the basis of a relationship with humankind in the act of creation. Just as Julian of Norwich understood Jesus to be revealing of a lost dimension of God, consideration of the experience of woman in light of the story of Creation could lead to a deeper revelation of God to individuals, to the Church and to the modern world and to the discovery of new aspects of the Divine plan not appreciated in earlier eras of human existence in the "world of the tree of the knowledge of good and of evil." The stories of the two caves, of "hearts" that are to be transformed and of the Holy Spirit in touch with our spirit could be enriched from this perspective.

When we reread our Biblical stories, reconsider our images of God and evaluate some of the practices and doctrines of our Christian tradition from the perspective of an analysis of some aspect of the experience of woman, we uncover a deeper appreciation of the significance of human life and of God's plan for it. For example, the bodily experience of woman captured somewhat morosely in the song's words, "only women bleed," has historically been the cause of negative treatment of women. Women themselves, even at the present time, do not, for the most part, find much positive value in this monthly ritual that spans nearly half their lifetime. "The curse," as young women referred to it in the 1950's, was an appropriate tag for an experience that set them apart from the males of their society and caused embarassment over their physical sexuality. Yet, this monthly ritual is a reminder of the generative possibilities of human existence and, if our religious tradition had puberty rites, the beginning of menstruation could be celebrated as a reminder of the continuing generativity of a God who is both mother and father. A feminine spirituality could celebrate this monthly reminder as a sign of the human ability to join with God in generative behavior, to continue Christ's redemptive activity in our immediate environment and age in history. This monthly ritual could also serve as a reminder to men that generativity is an important aspect of human existence revealed by God in many ways, one of which is the female body. The God of creation continues to remind us of a Divine plan in this experience of womankind.

Throughout human history women have been responsible for the care of the very young. When women today reflect on their experience, more often than not this caring tendency becomes apparent. How much of this caring is biologically determined we cannot now say. Though Alice Rossi's studies of endocrinology hint that there might be some biological basis for what appears to be a more finely tuned sense of caring in the female of the species, she is quick to point out that this does not mean that men do not or cannot be caring individuals, only that they might need to learn the depth of this tendency that comes more naturally to women. (cf. Alice Rossi, "A Bio-socio Perspective on Parenting", *Daedalus*, Spring, 1977). Here Rossi would seem to be in agreement with the Yahwist author who tells of the image of God being a man and a woman sharing their understanding of how it is to be a human being in such a way that this joint sharing reveals something of God, a God who cares about his creatures the way women care for the young. We can begin to see that much of Jesus' behavior, in shattering the expectations of his listeners, was based on a "caring" love, even unto death, not as a hero, but as a way toward a new "birth." No wonder Julian saw feminine aspects of Jesus.

People who are coming back to the Church are part of a generation that is being forced to evaluate their prior conceptions regarding male and female roles. The Church they come home to, if it is carrying on the work of Jesus, should be helping them recognize the transformation that must take place in the societal understanding of woman and woman's experience if men and women are to work toward the building of the kingdom where together they, like Adam and Eve, reflect the Divine Image.

Women returning to the Church, as well as men, need to be challenged by Jesus' call on the Sermon on the Mount to move beyond the cultural understanding of woman's role and evaluate their experiences in light of the God they find revealed both in the Scriptures and in their experiences. Though it is difficult to imagine many pastoral leaders who will challenge and encourage women in this task, it seems that the need to appreciate the womanly side of God is so vitally important that the homecomer who might have much to contribute to such a discussion ought to be made aware of the possibility of discovering God in the experience of woman.

The heirarchial Church needs to remember that "Wisdom has been proved right by *all her* children."

CHAPTER XV
Discernment of the Laity

SEVERAL stories introduce us to the problems of this chapter. The first is about a new pastor and associate pastor who are liturgical "purists." On their arrival at their new assignment they felt compelled to make changes in the Sunday liturgy. Within the first few months of their appearance on the parish scene, and with no understanding of how the parishoners felt about the liturgy, they initiated changes which added fifteen minutes on to the length of the Sunday Mass and de-emphasized some treasured moments. These changes did little more than add fifteen minutes of boredom. They were made in order to "purify" the ritual of a liturgy that the new priests felt too heavily emphasized the word aspect of liturgy. The result could have been predicted. People began leaving Mass early; the liturgical purists took to the altar to denounce this and to the doors of the Church to frown their disapproval at those who left early.

The second story deals with the Archdiocesan newspaper. Like many such papers this is the voice of the Archbishop and presents a one-sided view of what is going on in the Archdiocese and in the larger Church. The laity of the diocese had stopped subscribing to it in large numbers. So a directive was sent ordering each parish to fill a quota of a certain number of subscriptions. If the assigned number of parishoners did not voluntarily subscribe to the paper, additional copies would be sent directly to the rectory to be distributed as the rectory saw fit and the parish would be billed for its quota.

Another story, with which we are all familiar, deals with a synod of Bishops called to consider the issue of family. It resulted in a Papal statement which obviously has failed to take into account the actual experience of marriage and family life.

And then there is the university professor who maintains that the laity would not want to examine their faith in more depth. As students they aren't even interested in the courses in religion that are offered in the university and their willingness to delve into their faith is minimal. And there is the priest who maintains that perhaps we have listened to the laity too much and geared many of our pro-grams to what we have heard them say are their needs; for example, we offer them a program on parents and teen-agers and few of them show up.

And, of course, there is the story of the laity who come to a series of talks on human sexuality and are upset after the first session because the speaker has not given them rules that they in turn can pass on to their teen-agers concerning sexual behavior. It does not matter to them that their teen-agers would not listen to the rules even if the parents were to use "The Church says" as the rationale for specific behavior.

As these stories indicate, homecomers are returning to a Church where priests, hierarchy, scholars and the Pope think they know what is best for the laity in matters of religious life and moral behavior. The homecomers will also encounter laity who are content with those in authority making rules, especially when those rules refer to other people's behavior. The homecomer is not apt to find, in practice at least, much "listening" to the experience of the laity on the part of those in power positions within the Church or from academic theologians.

The gift of discernment, which is at one and the same time a gift and an obligation for the lay person, is seldom encouraged. When it does take place, the end results are either not heard or are ignored because, after all, the "elites" (and this includes lay people who are involved in positions of responsibility within the offical Church and are part of the academic study of religion) already know what is best. Thirty second pauses between Scriptural readings and Responsorial Psalms are instituted so the congregation will reflect on the meaning of the reading without ever investigating whether this is what the Congregation will do or wants to do at that particular time. The diocesan newspaper should be read by more people even though the laity has already expressed its disapproval of the paper by refusing voluntarily to subscribe to it. Perhaps the laity's opinion is not sought because their true response would prove so devastating to the elites' preconceived notions. How then could the elites find validity in their role?

The homecomers who have been attracted back to the religion of their beginnings—looking for a heritage, a place to pass on values to children, answers to questions about death and a religious community in which to explore the meaning of the various mysterious experiences of their lifes—have, in many instances, engaged in their own process of discernment. They have discovered "in their hearts" what it is their religious beliefs tell them about the meaning of life as they live it in their day-to-day encounters with the secular world. When they find the story of the two caves giving them the hope to survive and live with a certain sense of joy despite the tensions and anxieties of their life, they have made some links between their own experiences and the beliefs of the religious traditions to which they belong. The challenge they face is to enlarge upon this process of discernment so they may continually link the faith affirmed in the creeds proclaimed at Sunday liturgies with the life they live during the intervals between liturgies.

Althought it does not seem that Pope John Paul II has initiated any process for listening to this discernment of the laity, he has, on a number of occasions, emphasized the importance of the laity's participation in the Church's understanding of how it should respond to the situation of the contemporary world. In both his audience talks on the theology of the body and sexuality and in the apostolic exhortation, *Familiaris Consortio,* summing up his response to the synod on the family, the Pope speaks of the importance of the discernment of the laity.

For example, in his reflections on Christ's words concerning "adultery in the heart" which he interprets as a call to a transformation of the experience of sexuality, he writes:

Christ's words are severe. They demand from man that in the sphere in which relations with persons of the other sex are formed, he should have full and deep consciousness of his acts, and above all of interior acts; that he should be aware of the internal impulses of his 'heart,' so as to be able to distinguish them and qualify them maturely . . . he must learn, with perserverance and consistency, what is the meaning of the body, the meaning of masculinity and femininity. He must learn this not only through an objectifying abstraction (although this, too, is necessary), but above all in the sphere of the interior reactions of his own "heart". . . the interior man has been called by Christ to acquire a mature and complete evaluation, leading him to discern and judge the various movements of his very heart. And it should be added that this task *can* be carried out and is really worthy of man.

The process of discernment in our hearts called for by Jesus should lead to a deeper understanding of the meaning of sexuality written in our hearts at the very beginning of Creation.

The Pope later asks: How can and must the human who accepts Christ's words in the Sermon on the Mount act in the area of sexuality? How "can" we rely on our "inner self" as a source for interior and exterior acts? How "should" the values revealed in the Sermon on the Mount influence our desires and choices? As the Pope notes, various answers have been given to these questions in the past and present as found in ample literature on the topic. In addition, the Pope indicates:

> But also the ones worked out—certainly not without a link to the work of moralists and scientists—by individual men as authors and direct subjects of real morality, as co-authors of its history, on which there depends also the level of morality itself, its progress or its decadence.

Recognition that the level of morality itself depends on the answers that individuals give to the question of how they can and should act regarding their sexuality, and recognizing the importance of discerning and judging the answers to these questions in the individual heart certainly would require that the theologian and the moralist and the Church authority who make pronouncements on morality be attentive to the results of the discernment carried out by individuals.

This call for a listening to the experience of the laity does not mean that we find the complete answer to the religious questions of our times in the experience of the lay people. Rather, it is in the interaction of the experience and the tradition of religious beliefs that we begin to work out the answers to such questions as how can and should humans act regarding their sexuality (and other religious and moral questions). Individuals need a link with the work of moralists and scientists, but the work of the moralists and scientists has no influence if it does not address itself to the human "heart" both in its roots "in the image of God" and in its present historical situation. Failure of the Bishops participating in the Synod to publicly recognize the importance of sexual love in marriage exemplifies why statements by the elite of the Church which ignore the experience of concrete individuals will have little influence on the morality of the times. (We might also add that the failure of those Bishops who do recognize the need for keeping sexual love alive in a marriage to speak to this issue makes them responsible for setting up barriers for those who would see the Son and believe in him.)

The Pope elaborates on the understanding of discernment when he speaks about evangelical discernment in *Familiaris Consortio*, indicating that evangelical discernment is an orientation so that the entire truth and full dignity of marriage and the family may be preserved and realized:

This discernment is accomplished through the

sense of faith which is a gift that the Spirit gives
to all the faithful and is therefore the work of the
whole Church . . . the Church therefore does
not accomplish this discernment only through
the Pastors, who teach in the name and with
the power of Christ, but also through the laity . .

[who] moreover by reason of their particular
vocation have the specific role of interpreting
the history of the world in the light of Christ, in
as much as they are called to illuminate and
organize temporal realities according to the plan
of God, Creator and Redeemer.

The Pope then goes on to caution against the idea
that "the supernatural sense of faith" exists only in
the consensus of the faithful; its truth is not always
the same as the majority opinion. The Church does,
however, value sociological and statistical research
"when it proves helpful in understanding the
historical context in which pastoral action has to be
developed, when it leads to a better understanding
of the truth." This research alone, however, in itself
is not an expression of the sense of faith, and the
task of apostolic ministry is to promote the sense of
faith in all the faithful, and educate them to ever
more mature evangelical discernment. Even with
these cautions, however, the Pope is able to add:

Christian spouses and parents can and should
offer their unique and irreplaceable contribution

to the elaboration of an authentic evangelical discernment in the various situations and cultures in which men and women live their marriages and their family life. They are qualified for this role by their charism or specific gift, the gift of the Sacrament of Matrimony.

Unfortunately, this discernment of the laity for which they are qualified by the charism of marriage does not seem to have been listened to in the deliberations of the Bishops or in the proclamation of *Familiaris Consortio.* Though there are many good and positive statements in the exhortation, those sections on the transmission of life and the differences between contraception and rhythm and on the participation of divorced and remarried Catholics in the Eucharist only if they "take on themselves the duty to live in complete continence, that is by abstinence from the acts proper to married couples" are conclusions which show no awareness of the actual experience of sexuality and marriage in the modern world.

According to the Exhortation, theological reflection supposedly "in light of the experience of many [how many and under what circumstances, what sciences and whose theological reflection, we must ask] couples and of the data provided by the many human sciences" is able to perceive, "*the difference, both anthropological and moral* between contraception and recourse to the rhythm of the cycle." The ensuing argument for how the choice of the natural rhythm allows the couple to "recognize both the spiritual and corporal character of conjugal communion and to live the personal love with its requirement of fidelity" shows a complete lack of understanding of the development of intimacy in marital relationships. The Exhortation to theologians and pastors to "commit themselves to the task of illustrating ever more clearly the Biblical foundations, the ethical grounds and the personalistic "reasons" behind the Church's stand against birth control ignores the position of the lower clergy and a goodly number of theologians on this issue. The attempt to maintain that better knowledge of the rhythm method of birth regulation will lead to education in self control and the development of chastity fails to recognize the need for sexual intimacy in the development of a lifelong marital union. Too much control of sexual behavor, rather than lack of self control, is a problem for most marriages in the modern world. The witness of "many" (we do not know how "many" contributed to the defense of the feasibility of natural family planning) is certainly countered by the witness of the many more who reject it as a viable means of birth regulation.

The value of *Familiaris Consortio* is greatly diminished by the convoluted reasoning which attempts to support only the value of the rhythm method for the spiritual dimension of marriage. By ignoring the previously articulated vision of "two in one flesh" —a union which is social, psychological, sexual and religious and needs continual reinforcement in all areas—the statement ignores the lived experience of marriage in a modern technological society.

Unfortunately, the failure of the Bishops and of the Apostolic Exhortation to take into consideration the unique and irreplaceable contribution of Christian spouses to an authentic evangelical discernment creates a situation where newcomers are returning to a Church that is greatly divided on issues of sexual morality. They feel, correctly, that Church authorities are out of touch, if indeed they have ever been in touch with, the actual experience of marital living. So it appears the homecomers will find little inspiration for the task of discerning and judging in the heart through a conversation carried on between experience and the vision of human sexuality found in the stories of our faith. There is a disregard for the task of discernment of the laity in the Apostolic Exhortation and in the behavior of liturgists who don't bother to consider the experience of the laity and in diocesan officials who try to force the diocesan paper into people's homes and in theologians and university professors and all the other "elites" who continue their discussions about faith and doctrine, theology and Church structure, without any consideration for the religious needs of the faithful. This creates a situation that reminds us of children shouting to one another while they sit in the marketplace. If Church elites will not listen to the unique and irreplaceable contribution of the laity to an authentic evangelical discernment, they will be ineffectual in their attempt to offer an orientation that will help observe and realize the full dignity of human existence.

The homecomers who have been attracted back to the roots of childhood days, for the most part, choose to ignore the deliberations of the "elite." Their position is not unlike the position of the laity through most of the history of Christianity when faith was passed on from generation to generation primarily by means of story telling, and the majority of the faithful were not participants in the intellectual disputes of the small group of elites. Unfortunately, in today's world the faithful are aware and often-times embarassed by the behavior and pro-nouncements of the "elite." One would like to be proud of the Church one comes home to. Increas-ingly the "elites" with their uninformed stands on issues in the modern world and their hierarchical and clerical (in the pejorative sense of the word) stance put obstacles in the way of those who would hope to learn more of God through Jesus.

Homecomers however should bear in mind that they do have a special charism; they also have the promise that if they see the Son and believe in him they shall have eternal life and be raised up on the last day. Seeing the Son and believing in him requires that they hear his call for transformation of human existence and that they continue to try to interpret the history of the world in the light of Christ. It seems an unfair burden to place on the shoulders of the homecomers—this asking them to be vocal about the charism of discernment—yet a full appreciation of the story of Creation and of the two caves hopefully will encourage the homecomers to vocalize the results of their discernment. Pastoral ministers and parish communities who are open to a consideration of the charism of the laity in discussions of religious matters, would soon find much of the confusion of the children in the marketplace replaced by the harmony that can be found when people are working together toward developing the kingdom.

CHAPTER XVI
Conclusion

THE basic premise of this book has been that there are a sizable number of people in their late twenties, thirties and early forties who have come home to the Catholic Church, and that the best response to the religious needs of this group can be found in the development of a vision of life based on the images and stories of our tradition and linked to the practical experiences and lives of the homecomers. In addition, the reasons for coming home to the Church, as well as the critical issues in the lives of the homecomers, are both closely linked to the issues of marriage and family living. Sexual identity and the correct response to the fact of their human sexuality are crucial concerns for all people in this stage of the life cycle. We have indicated that most of those who come home will come home no matter what the official Church does or says. Still, there are signs that some might return earlier or more might return—and the Church as a whole might be enriched by their contribution—if those in positions of authority in the Church (the elites) would develop an appreciation of the unique and unrepeatable contribution these homecomers have to make to the Catholic Community. The homecomers need pastoral ministers who will listen to their position as well as challenge them to discern and judge in their "hearts," to contribute the fruits of their discernment

to the ongoing evangelical discernment of the full
Christian community.

John Shea maintains that the critical need for the
Church in the eighties is the development of a reflective faith. The problem most pastoral ministers face
with this need to develop a reflective faith in
themselves and in their people, including the
homecomers, is that, in the past we did not always
appreciate the ways in which we linked our ordinary
experiences with the stories of faith so that many of
them became extraordinary experiences, that is,
experiences of God. We did not, in the past, understand the role of religion in our lives; we did not see
how many of the religious practices, which were
discarded after the second Vatican Council, helped
us link our own experiences to the stories of our
faith. In them we found the basic beliefs about God
and about a God-humankind relationship flushed
out in stories of God. Our examination of the
phenomenon of the homecomer leads us to conclude with some recommendations for how the
Church might begin to profit from insights into the
role of religion in the experience of all of wisdom's
children.

1) All levels of the elite (Popes, Bishops,
theologians, pastors and pastoral workers) need to
develop appropriate processes for incorporating the
unique and unrepeatable charism of the discernment
of the faithful into discussions of and decisions on
religious and moral issues. Although sociological

and statistical researchers alone are not sufficient for gaining a sense of the faithful, they do point a way toward further study. Other ways of "listening" to all the faithful and to the particular needs of specific individuals and groups must be developed. Homecomers, for the most part, will need to be encouraged to join in any organized discussion of religious issues but when critical areas of their lives are being examined, some undoubtedly will respond.

2) Pastoral leaders need to learn how to spark the religious imagination of the homecomers, much as it was sparked when they were young, by the stories of the two caves. As we noted in *Parish, Priest and People,* the pastoral minister needs to exercise his / her creative imagination and develop the art of story telling. A creative re-telling of the stories of our faith through liturgy and especially through good homilies and through various art forms will awaken in the hearts and minds of the faithful an awareness of God's presence in their ordinary experiences. These ordinary experiences become extraordinary possibilities with the discovery of the Divine.

3) Professional Church persons should develop an appreciation for what religion means in the life of the ordinary person. The concerns of priests and the hierarchy with Church structure and those of theologians, the Curia and the Pope, with doctrine and morality, simply are not concerns of the ordinary person in the pews. The homecomer has

come back to the Church because it is the community which celebrates the values that help one
live a life of meaning in a world that, at times, seems
meaningless. Of course, the beliefs of the Catholic
faith and tradition are the basis of these values and
need to be interpreted anew for each generation.
But the homecomer's membership in the Catholic
Church does not depend upon the outcome of
theological and moral discussions. Rather it depends
upon the religious community and its ability to keep
alive the values that flow from a belief in a Creator
God who love us, his Divine Son who redeemed us
and a Holy Spirit who continues his presence in the
world. God's plan for human life, which helps us
cope with the difficulties we encounter, encourages
us to celebrate the joys we encounter, encourages us
to celebrate the joys we experience and challenges
us ever anew to cooperate in continuing God's
presence in the world. This belief is at the root of the
attractiveness of religion to the homecomer. The
organized Church needs to recognize this role of
religion in the life of the faithful and develop ways of
increasing an appreciation for the implications of this
in their lives.

   4) Since the issue of sexuality, the fact that human
beings come in male and female varieties, influences
every aspect of our life and since misunderstandings
about the meaning of human sexualtiy cause critical
problems in the lives of the homecomers, those who
minister to these homecomers must find new ways

of proclaiming a vision of sexuality based on our religious traditions. Homecomers believe that the official Church is insensitive to the issue of human sexuality. They have, for the most part, given up any hope of the Church offering them a means for transforming the societal understanding of sexuality which often causes them great distress. Most pastoral ministers realize their congregation is not listening to the official Church position on issues of sexuality. Many of those ministers are not even sure of their own sexual identity and feel that it is an area best left untouched in religious discussions, thereby robbing the faithful of a positive vision of human sexuality. This means that a very large portion of the homecomers will not hear of the positive plan of God for man and woman and will be unable to relate their religious beliefs to this crucial part of their lives.

5) Pastoral ministers and the hierarchy must struggle to regain the Church's credibility in the area of woman's role in modern society. They must fight against the impression of negative attitudes towards women conveyed by the Church's position on ordination. All levels of the Church must immediately take concrete actions to eliminiate discrimination against women. Words are not enough. "My sisters and brothers," and "women and men" and vocal support for the ordination of women are meaningless from people who in their day-to-day dealings with women tend to fall back on stereotyping. Clergy and laity alike need to recognize the expectations

they have for women in today's world, especially those in the age bracket of the homecomers. Also, there should be an evaluation of the contribution women make to the Church and to religion. Often the impression is that the Church has no need for their talents other than at the level of "women's work." Everyone in our society today, men and women alike, must struggle to overcome the stereotyping tendencies that have been part of our culture certainly since its historical beginning. Those who are concerned about the homecomers recognize that about half of them are women and many of these are turned off by official Church responses to women's experience.

6) And to the homecomers we would say, you are among those who are given to Jesus by the Father. You who believe in Jesus will return with him to the Father on the last day. You are welcomed back into the Church by Jesus and the Father. Your experiences of God which have led you back to the Church are vitally important to the Church's mission to proclaim the message of God in the modern world. You are part of the Church, one of wisdom's children. You are a new phenomenon in the Church but your message about the importance of religious values is a hopeful message and one that you should consider sharing with the rest of the faithful. The Church you have come home to is a human and fallible institution always in need of challenge to be faithful to its mission. Your presence renews that challenge and gives us hope there will be a response.